REFORMATION

A play

By James Martin Charlton

Published by Playdead Press 2019

© James Martin Charlton 2019

James Martin Charlton has asserted his rights under the
Copyright, Design and Patents Act, 1988, to be identified
as the author of this work.

A CIP catalogue record for this book is available from the
British Library.

ISBN 978-1-910067-80-2

Playdead Press
www.playdeadpress.com

Reformation was first performed at The White Bear Theatre, Kennington on 25th June 2019, presented by JMC Fire.

CAST (in order of appearance)

Ava	**Alice De-Warrenne**
Gretel	**Imogen Smith**
Benno	**Adam Sabatti**
Joachim	**Simeon Willis**
Albert	**Matt Ian Kelly**
Cranach	**Jason Wing**
Lucas	**Ram Gupta**

Directed by **Janice Dunn**

Designed by **Lucy Bond**

Lighting by **Anna Reddyhoff**

Produced by **Nayomi Roshini** with **Lucia Cox**

Production Management by **Andrew Roberts**

Stage Management by **Reece J Marchant**

Trailer by **Dariush Asadi & Patrycja Lisowska**

Publicity Photography by **Max Harrison & Mohib Anis**

Graphic Design by **Guillem Matallanas Riba**

PR by **Chris Hislop**

Marketing by **My Theatre Mates**

Thanks to David Cottis and all at ScriptTank for their dramaturgical input; to Christian Durham for his useful feedback on the script; Ergin Cavusoglu, Paul Cobley, Vida Midgelow, Carole-Anne Upton and the ACI Faculty Research Fund at Middlesex University for helping to fund the production; and to Michael Kingsbury and all at the White Bear Theatre.

Special Thanks to our "Church Patron" Robin Fairfield for his generous support.

THE CREATIVE TEAM

James Martin Charlton | Writer

James is a dramatist, director and academic. His plays include *Fat Souls* and *Coming Up* (Warehouse Theatre, Croydon); *ecstasy + Grace* (Finborough Theatre); *Desires of Frankenstein* (Open Air, Regents Park & Pleasance, Edinburgh); *The World & his Wife, I Really Must be Getting Off* (The White Bear); *Coward* (Just Some Theatre Co.) He has written two short pieces for The Miniaturists, *Fellow Creature* and *Battis Boy* (Arcola Theatre*)*. His recent play *Been on the Job Too Long* has been produced three times since 2015 (at TheatreN16, the North London Literary Festival, and the Talos Festival of Science Fiction Theatre). He wrote an adaptation of *The Pilgrim's Progress* under commission by the RSC, and his biographical play about William Blake, *Divine Vision*, was performed at Swedenborg Hall.

He has directed a number of contemporary plays, including *Gob*, *Bumps* (King's Head), *Plastic Zion* (White Bear), *Histrionics* (Underbelly, Edinburgh). His production of *Revolution Farm* by James Kenworth after Orwell played at Newham City Farm in 2014; *A Splotch of Red: Keir Hardie in West Ham* toured east London in 2016.

He has written and directed two short films, *Apeth* (2007) and *Academic* (2011). He wrote screenplays for the shorts *Emotional Tribunal* and *Best Shot*. He recently filmed his play *Fellow Creature* for 360° video, as part research project into the medium which resulted in the 2019 article 'VR and the dramatic theatre: are they fellow creatures?' in the peer-reviewed *International Journal of Performance Arts and Digital Media*.

He has lectured at UEL and Birkbeck and is Head of Department of Media at Middlesex University.

Janice Dunn | Director

Janice is an experienced theatre director who has worked extensively in the UK and Europe throughout her career. She is also a writer who produces scripts in both English and Danish. Janice provides her own movement direction, and in the past, choreography, for most of the shows she directs.

Highlights of her career include *The Force of Change* (Royal Court Theatre), *Small Miracle* (Tricycle Theatre), *Catastrophic Sex Music* (Theatre 503 / Latitude Festival)

Sound of a Hammer (Birmingham Rep), *Goldfish* (Liverpool Everyman), *Absurd Person Singular* (Oldham Coliseum), *Skuespillerakademiet* (The Actors Academy, Copenhagen), *Chicago, Guys and Dolls, It's a Lovely Day Tomorrow, Godspell, From a Jack to a King, Boyband* (Belgrade Theatre, Coventry), *Oh What a Lovely War, Arturo Ui The Musical, The Europeans* (Mercury, Colchester). She has written and directed 20 years' worth of pantomimes for Belgrade Theatre, Mercury Theatre, Spa Centre Leamington, and De Montfort Hall Leicester.

Janice spent 12 years delivering residential creative development and training programmes for participants from Europe and beyond, for ages from 14 to 80 years (Luxemburg / Belgium). She was an associate artist on the ACE funded Creative Partnerships Programme, for the West, and East, Midlands regions, delivering bespoke creative projects for young people, which also trained teachers in new skills. She was the UK director representative on the EU funded PLOTS Project. This brought six countries together, to create and tour three new works throughout Europe, with multi-national casts.

Lucy Bond | Designer

Lucy graduated from the Theatre Design course at Nottingham Trent University in July 2018 where she achieved a First-Class Honours degree. During her degree she designed the set for *Lysistrata* written by Aristophanes and directed by Martin Berry at The Lakeside Arts Centre.

Since Graduating she has been a design assistant for Verity Quinn on Theatre Rites' *Big Up*, Wardrobe Assistant at LaplandUK 2018, Assistant to the design team on The Guildford Shakespeare Company's production of *Measure 4 Measure* designed by Neil Irish, Wardrobe Maintenance on Mathew Bourne's *Swan Lake*, and is incredibly excited to be designing *Reformation*.

Anna Reddyhoff | Lighting

Anna has been working within the entertainment industry for almost 10 years after graduating in 2010. Her early work was predominantly music based, before spending several years on the touring musical theatre scene. She is thrilled to be working on the creative team on *Reformation*.

Other current and upcoming productions include; *The Lion, The Witch and The Wardrobe* (Lichfield Garrick Theatre); *The Re-Birth of Meadow Rain* (Edinburgh Fringe). Previous lighting design credits include; *Flinch* (The Old Red Lion); *Emilia* (Vaudeville Theatre / Associate LD to Zoe Spurr); *Heart The Play* (The Vaults, London); Sara Pascoe: *Lads Lads Lads* (Wyndham's Theatre); Tim Vine: *Sunset Milk Idiot* (Eventim Hammersmith Apollo); *One Man Two Guvnors* (Lichfield Garrick); *Elf The Musical Junior* (Friary Theatre Lichfield); *Once Upon a Mattress* (Lichfield Garrick); *Rent* (A3 Arena). Other selected credits include; Re-Lighter for *Transporting*

Live (UK Tour – Seabright Productions); Chief Electrician for Secret Cinema's *Moulin Rouge; This Is My Family* (UK Tour / Sheffield Theatres); Deputy Chief Electrician for (*Chitty Chitty Bang Bang* (UK Tour); *Anything Goes* (UK Tour); Deputy Head of Lighting and Video for *Hairspray* (UK Tour).

Nayomi Roshini | Producer

Nayomi is a member of the Arcola Women's Company and regularly participates in community theatre workshops held at the Arcola Theatre including a recent course on Producing Theatre. She produced the play *A Splotch of Red: Keir Hardie in West Ham* by James Kenworth which toured in East London in 2016. She also produced the short film *HOST* directed by Joe Cohen in 2016.

She graduated in 2011 with a BA in Film Video and Interactive arts and just recently completed her MA in Film. She is interested in both independent theatre and film and has increasingly becoming more interested in directing performance. She wrote her MA dissertation on the use of improvisation in film as a tool to deepen characterisation. She currently works in the Media Department at Middlesex University as an academic assistant where she has continued to develop her filmmaking practice through her work as a production manager on various short film projects led by the department and other students. Her filmmaking practice as a short film director has mostly focused on exploring female subjectivity and the gaze.

Andrew Roberts | Production manager

Andrew began his career in entertainment in North London's Stallion Hi-Fi Sound System, in which he performed under the name Sqwidli Junya. The climax of his performing career was playing to an appreciative audience of thousands at Notting Hill Carnival.

He has since built a career in personnel management and HR for major retailers. He has recently completed a BA (Sociology) at Middlesex University, where his dissertation scrutinised what being British means to Britons and how tolerant we are of diverse cultures.

His previous production management experience was for the tour of *A Splotch of Red: Keir Hardie in West Ham*, which toured to several Newham libraries and Community Links in Plaistow.

THE CAST

Alice De-Warrenne | Ava

Alice graduated from The Guildford School of Acting (GSA) in 2015.

She has spent the past year touring the UK and Ireland with the first stage adaptation of the CBeebies show *Bing Live* – playing the role of Coco. Other recent theatre credits include *Wrecked* (The VAULT Festival); *The Unfortunate Trial of Robin Goodfellow* (Greenwich Theatre); *Santa's Invitation* (Ductac, Dubai); *Jack and the Giant* (UAE Tour); *Under My Thumb* (Greenwich Theatre, New Diorama and Edinburgh Fringe Festival); *Hay Fever* (Upstairs at The Gatehouse / UK Tour); *Alice in Wonderland*; *The Gingerbread Man* (UAE tour); *A Night at the Bar(d)* (Floods Tavern); *Under My Thumb* (rehearsed reading, Greenwich Theatre); *The Wind and the Willows* (Waterloo East) and *True West* (Ivy Arts Centre).

Credits whilst training include A *Midsummer Night's Dream*; *The Crucible*; *A Doll's House* (GSA) and *The Children's Hour* (Ivy Arts Centre).

Alice is delighted to be appearing in this production, especially as it gives a voice to one of the many voiceless women of history.

Ram Gupta | Lucas

Ram trained with the National Youth Theatre. His previous theatre work includes *Wherever I Lay My Head* (National Youth Theatre / Coram); *I (Never) Did* (Redgates Theatre) and *Papercut* (Quilliam / Angry Bairds / Tour).

Screen work includes *The Distants* (London Live – Endemol Shine Talent Award); *A Necessary Evil* (ITV); *Sorry* (Island Records / Untold) and *Schism* (Dir: Hayden Munt).

Matt Ian Kelly | Albert

Matt trained at ALRA.

Theatre credits include *What's Wrong with Angry?* (Oval House / BAC); *I am Oscar Wilde* (Croydon Warehouse); *London Life – The Secret Kinks Of World War II* (The Hope Theatre). Matt has worked extensively with Les Enfant Terribles, originating the role of Lucifer in *Immaculate* (UK / International Tours) and *The Terrible Infants* (UK Tour & Holden Street Theatre during the Adelaide Festival). For Greenwich Theatre, he appeared as Bob Hull in the award winning tour of *The Temperamentals* (Dublin Festival & Courtyard Theatre, Hereford); as Countess Marie Laure De Tily in *Lilies* (Dublin / Greenwich Theatre); in Ian Lindsay's *Chinese Whispers*, and co-wrote and devised *Jennifer Skylark And The Seagull's Handbook*, a site specific children's piece created in conjunction with Powderkeg. Matt has also worked extensively with O&Co Productions at The Kenton Theatre in Henley On Thames, starring in the pantos *Jack and The Beanstalk* and *Sleeping Beauty*, appearing in both in the role of 'Dame / Nurse Trott' and starring alongside Peter Duncan in *The Three Musketeers*.

Screen credits include *V*oicing the role of Charles Dickens for the documentary film *Fallen Women* for the Derek Jarman Lab; *Tomorrow People* (Big Finish Productions); *Kira: A Tale of Love in the Darkness* (Bushey Hill Productions) and the role of Howard in *Limbo* (Andre Llewellyn Films). Last year, Matt took the recurring role of 'Colonel Sage' in *Zombies, Run! Season 7* for 'Six to Start'.

Adam Sabatti | Benno

Adam trained at Drama Studio London.

Theatre credits include *Living Latino* (The Kings Head Theatre); *First Time For Adults: A Musical* (Market Theatre); *It's A Long Walk Home Tonight* (Bread & Roses Theatre); *F*cking Foreigners* (South Hill Park) and *Barred Freedom* (The Cockpit Theatre).

He has also done rehearsed readings at The Sam Wanamaker Playhouse, Sackler Studios (both as part of Read Not Dead) & at The Hope Theatre, London.

Short film credits include *My Sweet Lord*, *Spectrum*, *Red Berkeley*, *Then Anthropocene*, *Happy Birthday You Loser*, *Foxhole & Block*. TV credits include *Small World*.

Imogen Smith | Gretel

Theatre credits include *Love and Friendship* (Omnibus Clapham); *Out of the Mouth of the Parrett* (Theatre Mélange); *Sunday Readings in the Park* (Park Theatre); *Broadbent* (Theatre West at Bristol Old Vic); *Bed Among the Lentils* (Northcott Exeter); *To Kill a Mockingbird* (York Theatre Royal & UK Tour); *Palace of the End* directed by Jessica Swale (Arcola Theatre); *The Mona Lisas* (Theatre Mélange / Teatrul Ariel Romania); *The Time of the Tortoise* (Theatre 503); *Coriolanus* directed by Steven Berkoff (Festival Theatre Edinburgh); *L'Ascensore* (Pete Brooks Company); *The Winter's Tale* (Royal Theatre Northampton); *Lysistrata* (Edinburgh Festival / White Bear Theatre).

Film credits include *Care As You Are* (Joanna Proctor); *Renaud* (Yann Gorriz); *Between the Silence* (Luke Moss); *Angel's Charms* (Christopher Clarke).

TV credits includes *Off the Beaten Track* (ITV); *Trollied* (Roughcut TV); *Meet the Humans* (BBC World).

Audio & Radio credits include *Stephen Fry's Victorian Secrets* (Audible); *Nothing Sacred* (Resonance FM); *The Hysterical Method of Conception* (Radio 4 Woman's Hour); *Saving Grace* (White House Sound).

Simeon Willis | Joachim

Simeon trained at Bretton Hall.

Theatre credits include *Constance – The Amazing Mrs Oscar Wilde* (Canal Café Theatre); *Road* (Broadway Studio Theatre / Tabard Theatre); *The Future* (Pentameters); *Book of Little Things* (Oval House Theatre); *Wuthering Heights; Romeo and Juliet* (Wycombe Swan); *The Usual Suspects* (Colchester Mercury / Riverside Studios / UK Tour).

TV & Film credits include *Mr Selfridge* (ITV); *Hetty Feather* (CBBC), *The Gatehouse* (Lionsgate); *Second Spring* (Late Autumn Films); *Narcopolis* (Altitude); *Arcadia* (Big View Media / Kaleidoscope); *The Rizen* (GoldFinch Entertainment); *Egomaniac* (Hex Media); *50 Kisses* (Living Spirit / Miggins Films / Puzzle Pictures); *Headlock Security* (Dogsky Films); *Castles Made Of Sand* (5A Films); *The Ipanema File* (Fighting Badgers Ltd); *Third Contact* (Body Double Productions); *Borges And I* (Indivision Films). Short Films include *The Messenger* (Pixelform Studios); *Two Strangers Meet Five Times* (Double M Films Ltd); *The Choke* (MWP Digital Media).

Jason Wing | Cranach

Jason trained at Drama Centre.

He made his professional stage debut in director Jonathan Miller production of *The Beggar's Opera*. Theatre credits include *All About Edgar Allen Poe, A Fight At The Opera, A Midsummer Night's Dream, Burnt Oak, Coffee in Memphis, Hamlet, Many Roads to Paradise, Mojo, Orpheus Descending, What the Butler Saw*.

Film credits include *Dead and Awake, Hooligan Legacy, Lost A Girl, Richard the Third, Rise of the Footsoldier, Robin Hood the Rebellion, Soldier Of War, The Antwerp Dolls, The Ballad Of Mulla And Mullins, Transhuman, Velvet Thompson, Zoo Head, 24 Little Hours*.

Voice credits include lead voiceover in *Filthy Lucre* for Sony Playstation.

JMC Fire

JMC Fire is an independent production company formed to promote, produce and increase awareness of the plays of James Martin Charlton.

Since the mid-1980s, Charlton has written a series of plays which use a poetic sensibility and rich, theatrical language to tell stories about characters who might otherwise be ignored. He puts at the centre of his plays such characters as an overweight, lonely jobseeker (*Fat Souls*), a teenage vandal and his concerned teacher (*Coming Up*), a pimp and an underage rent boy (*ecstasy + GRACE*), a socially awkward gay misfit (*I Really Must be Getting Off*), an actor sexually harassed by a star (*Coward*), a barman framed for a murder (*Been on the Job Too Long*). He puts these unlikely protagonists at the heart of stories which hint at universal myths and folktales.

Charlton writes contemporary plays which deal with strikingly current themes and action within conventions drawn from varied eras of theatre – masks, verse, asides and soliloquies; medieval, well-made or Renaissance multi-plot structures. This practice places the characters and their stories in a unique theatrical world which removes them from the trappings of social realism and which might allow us to see them afresh.

JMC Fire will premiere new Charlton texts and revive his earlier plays. The company will give new and emerging artists and skilled practitioners the chance to encounter and create exciting new theatre from these texts.

The Team
Artistic Director | **James Martin Charlton**
Artistic Associates | **Andrew Roberts / Nayomi Roshini**

White Bear Theatre

History

The White Bear Theatre took off in 1989, founded by Michael Kingsbury, and focuses on new writing and lost classics. It exists to nurture and develop exceptional new and existing talent and offer a space where risks can be taken.

People who have cut their teeth at The White Bear Theatre include: Joe Penhall, Emily Watson, Mehmet Ergen, Tamzin Outhwaite, Kwame Kwei Armah, Vicky Featherstone, Torben Betts, and Lucinda Coxon.

The White Bear Theatre has also developed and hosted work by a new generation of theatre makers including Verity Bargate Winner Vicky Jones, Blanche McIntyre, The Ugly Sisters, and Simon Evans. Former White Bear Theatre Associates include Adam Spreadbury-Maher and Box of Tricks Theatre.

Michael Kingsbury is on the board of The Society Of Independent Theatres which represents leading Off-West-End theatres.

The White Bear Theatre has recently undergone extensive upgrades including full air conditioning, brand new lighting and sound equipment and benefits from excellent sound proofing of the theatre.

Awards

The White Bear Theatre has received numerous awards including Off West End Awards in 2011 and 2012, and the Mark Marvin / Peter Brook Award for 2012/13. Other awards include Time Out Best Fringe Venue, Peter Brook Empty Space Award for Best Up and Coming Venue, Carling London

Fringe Awards for Best Actor & Best Production, and the Fringe Report Award for Outstanding Achievement.

Transfers

Our transfers have included the recent production of *Inigo* transferring to The Pleasance, *The Confessions of Gordon Brown* and *Madness in Valencia* both to Trafalgar Studio 2. and *Round the Horne... Revisited* which played in the West End for 18 months, completed 3 first-class tours and was chosen for the Royal Variety Performance.

The London première of John Osborne's second play *Personal Enemy* transferred to the prestigious Brits Off-Broadway Festival in New York, and other transfers include *Muswell Hill* to Park Theatre, *The Duchess of Malfi* to Southwark Playhouse, and *Count Oederland* to the Arcola Theatre. The recent Offie Nominated production of *Out There on Fried Meat Ridge Road* also transferred to Trafalgar 2 in May 2017.

The Team

Artistic Director | **Michael Kingsbury**
Associate Director | **Georgia Leanne Harris**
Literary Associate | **David Cottis**

Taken from Life – History, Art, and Truth

Since (roughly) the invention of photography, it's been a commonplace of art criticism that the exact representation of visible reality isn't part of a painter's job. The younger medium does it better, and most people reading this would no sooner be caught saying 'But it doesn't look that like!' than they would 'But that poem doesn't rhyme!'.

At the same time, it's become a lot more common to expect a dramatic work to do the job of the historian – as I write this, I'm surrounded by articles about the historical accuracy (or otherwise) of the TV series *Chernobyl*. This is quite a modern concern; as far as we know, no one in Shakespeare's audience complained about his misrepresentation of the facts when dealing with Richard III or Macbeth.

James Martin Charlton calls *Reformation* 'speculative fiction'. Lucas Cranach, his son, and their aristocratic and religious patrons were all real people, and their attitudes and relationships in the play are truthful to what we know about their real-life counterparts. The working classes, inevitably, leave less behind them, and these characters, and their interactions, are fictional. In the same way that science-fiction authors will allow themselves one alteration of the laws of physics, the author has included one historical fabrication – Renaissance artists like Cranach the Elder didn't generally use life models, seeing their work as the embodiment of an ideal rather than an individual.

The other function of painting that photography has mostly usurped is, of course, the depiction of naked flesh. Renaissance artists gave their patrons a lot of skin, whether in the form of a curvaceous Suzanna being ogled by her elders on both sides of the canvas, or a buff St. Sebastian awaiting the arrows' multiple penetrations. Frequently, the subject matter would be something that allowed the viewer to both eat and retain his cake – a painting of David and Bathsheba (or, indeed, the Rape of Lucrece) provides an opportunity to act as both moralist and voyeur, like a scandal-sheet journalist, or a Renaissance Cecil B. de Mille.

As with all historical plays, *Reformation* is really about the present. Although the play's conception preceded the Time's Up and MeToo movements, it shares their concerns with the complex interrelations between power, art and sexuality. In this respect, it's a cousin to the same author's *Coward*, seen at the White Bear in 2013, in which the predator and artist were the same person, and which played a similar game with history, moving an event from Nöel Coward's later life to his pre-war imperial period.

In *Reformation*, artist, patron and model form a triangle of dependency and desire. Each of them has something that at least one of the others wants, and is willing to pay for, whether in cash, flesh, status or skill. In this play's world, like that of Faust, you are what you can sell – the challenge is to get a decent price.

David Cottis
Literary Associate
White Bear Theatre
June 2019

Reformation is dedicated to Nayomi Roshini. I am eternally grateful for her tireless work, dedication and faith.

FIGURES IN THE DRAMA

CRANACH the elder, *a merchant and a painter*

JOACHIM I Nestor, *Elector of Brandenburg*

ALBERT of Hohenzollern, *Archbishop of Mainz*

LUCAS Cranach the younger, *apprentice painter*

BENNO, *assistant to Joachim*

GRETEL, *mother to Benno*

AVA, *Benno's niece*

NOTES

Lucas Cranach the Elder was one of the first great Protestant Artists of the Reformation. A close friend to Martin Luther, he used his Art to propagate the new Protestant theology. Yet he continued to work under commission for the non-Reformed Electors and Bishops in the German lands, painting portraits and moral scenes based on the Bible, Mythology and Antique history. The play is a speculation – a dream – on his working relationship with these un-Reformed men. And on those deemed not important enough to feature in Art history books...

*

The play is set in Berlin-Cölln in 1529 (and, the last scene, 1540) but don't make too much of that. The language is deliberately anachronistic, as if to take the story somewhat into our time. A designer might similarly introduce anachronisms; in fact, it's probably worth while doing so...

*

"We are all prostitutes" – The Pop Group.

*

This is the text as of the first day of rehearsals.

Act One

1

(A kind of 1529. A sparsely furnished room in a peasant's hovel within the gates of the city. On display, a large and kitsch effigy of the Virgin Mary. A young girl, AVA and her grandmother, GRETEL, both anxious. AVA peeks out of the window, curtain-twitching.)

AVA: I ought to be used to his disappearances.

GRETEL: Come away from the window.

(GRETEL pulls AVA away from the window.)

AVA: You're in a funny mood today.

GRETEL: Am not.

AVA: Chewing your lip like it's fat on a shank.

GRETEL: Don't feel well.

AVA: You were weeping this morning.

GRETEL: Me, weeping?

AVA: Before I was up.

GRETEL: Had a funny tummy.

AVA: Where's my Dad?

(GRETEL involuntarily weeps.)

                You see.

GRETEL: He's gone. Away. Your uncle did tell you.

AVA: Uncle's in the doldrums too.

GRETEL: Forget about your Dad.

(*GRETEL picks up a cloth and starts darning.*)

AVA: Dad says you sit there darning holes all day because you're an hole. Hole for your husband. Hole for your sons to push out of.

GRETEL: What does he expect you'll be?

AVA: Free.

GRETEL: You're free of him now. The only help you can expect -

(*GRETEL makes her way over to the sideboard.*)

AVA: Neither you nor uncle...

(*GRETEL picks up the effigy of Mary.*)

GRETEL: Our Lady.

(*AVA stares at the statue.*)

                Get on your knees.

(*AVA pauses a moment, then sinks to her knees. GRETEL joins her, kneeling next to her with the statue in front of them.*)

                Holy Mary, help the miserable, strengthen the discouraged, comfort the sorrowful...

(*AVA joins in.*)

BOTH: ...pray for your people, plead for the clergy, intercede for all women sacred to God.

(GRETEL gets down to darning. She is weeping. AVA turns back to the window.)

*

2

(The walls of the room disappear and a circular, roadside gallows is revealed. BENNO, a rough peasant fellow in courtier's livery, looks up at a corpse on the roundel, a man in his late thirties; a circle of other corpses dangle, children and adults. BENNO addresses the corpse.)

BENNO: Always hanging around, work too good for you. You're hanging around now, ain't you? Always wanting to hang out with some gang. You're hanging with a bad lot now, ain't you?

(The wind blows the corpses and they dance, as if in response. BENNO gestures to the corpse of a boy which has fallen against BENNO's brother.)

You got a son now? Little bit of rotting flesh of your flesh. Would've been nice, a nephew. Instead...

(Wind blows the corpse. It seems to dance angrily.)

Don't fret. I'll do my best for the girl. Better than you ever did. Best bit of parenting you ever did, getting hung.

(BENNO looks forlornly at the gallows. A sound. Low rumble, getting closer. BENNO turns. Looks down the road. Louder. Getting louder. Horses hooves and wheels. A carriage thunders past

*the gallows, on its way into Berlin-Cölln; perhaps the sound of a
steam locomotive somewhere under this. BENNO watches it go.*)

Someone's in a rush.

(*He looks at the fresh corpse again.*)

Bone to pick with you.

(*He laughs.*)

You hear that. I said, bone to...

(*He stops laughing.*)

My bestest wooden top. Daddy whittled a face on
it. I danced it on tables, raced it round the
scullery, dived it off chairs. Bedded it in my arms,
my baby Jesus. "Where's it gone?" Never able to
keep your hands off anything, were you? Bigger
than me. Dad had other things to take care of.
Took something off someone bigger than you.
Glad he's took care of you. Glad!

(*BENNO weeps like a child. Church bells from Berlin-Cölln ring.
BENNO looks up.*)

Better be getting off.

(*He notices the wood on the ground. He looks around, shifty.*)

Handy for the fire. Not a wasted journey...

(*He quickly gathers up the wood and fills his basket. When
finished, he goes back to the gallows, grabs the foot of his brother's
corpse. Stands frozen in the agony of the struggle to accept this. He
accepts it. No other choice, really.*)

Say hello if I'm passing eh brother?

(*He chuckles bitterly then turns back to Berlin-Cölln, walks off home. The wind again wakes the dancers to a few groundless steps of their round.*)

*

3

(*The Grand hall in the Berliner Schloss; the roost of an old Catholic aristocracy. JOACHIM, Elector of Brandenburg greets his brother ALBERT, Archbishop of Mainz.*)

JOACHIM: Brother.

ALBERT: Don't you brother me! It's time you got your roads sorted. What do you do with the tax? There's more to pomp, I'll have you know, than –

JOACHIM: Pomp?

ALBERT: More to luxury than swanning around your Schloss admiring your hangings.

JOACHIM: He has the temerity –

ALBERT: Admiring your maid servants.

JOACHIM: Compare our coats.

(*ALBERT flounces.*)

Mine is black, unostentatious.

ALBERT: Bear fur unostentatious?

JOACHIM: Gets ever so nippy here in the sticks.

ALBERT: Cold as a Proddie's kiss.

JOACHIM: You're all right in your ermine-ruffed robes, swathed in your red velvet.

ALBERT: I simply display the glory of my office. The glory of the Church. The glory of God.

JOACHIM: God's certainly looking gloriously healthy.

ALBERT: Miracle, journey I've had.

JOACHIM: It's good to see you.

ALBERT: Talk about a boneshaker. If I didn't have duties here. A consecration –

JOACHIM: Give us a kiss.

ALBERT: The odd high mass –

JOACHIM: Hug me, Alby!

ALBERT: Care of your soul.

JOACHIM: Don't come on account of me.

(ALBERT presents his hand to JOACHIM, who kisses it passionately, holds it.)

Would you like a drink?

ALBERT: Thought you'd never ask.

(JOACHIM rings a bell.)

I had a companion in my carriage.

28

JOACHIM: You don't have to carry them all the way from Mainz, we've plenty of altar boys.

ALBERT: A painter.

JOACHIM: Oh.

(*Enter BENNO.*)

The Archbishop will drink

(*To ALBERT*) Beer?

ALBERT: Wine.

JOACHIM: White?

ALBERT: Red.

(*JOACHIM screws up his face.*)

God doesn't come cheap.

JOACHIM: Beer for me.

(*Exit BENNO.*)

ALBERT: New man?

JOACHIM: Marvellous useful.

ALBERT: Ill countenanced.

JOACHIM: I don't employ servants for their looks, unlike -

ALBERT: Not the men, no.

JOACHIM: I hung his brother this morning. They're extra faithful once you've strung up a member of the clan. Feel they've something to prove.

ALBERT: (*Nods*) Our peasants have behaved since we put down their revolt.

JOACHIM: God rules our hearts by fear.

ALBERT: You have been listening.

(*Enter BENNO. He hands out drinks.*)

The painter's to work for you?

JOACHIM: Comes highly recommended.

(*ALBERT drinks, rolling his tongue around his mouth and smacking his lips*)

ALBERT: Very piquant.

(*BENNO retreats but does not leave the room.*)

The painter has unhealthy friends.

JOACHIM: Whenever I travel in Italy I – don't care about his friends! – whenever I go to a Medici gaff, they're showing off all these paintings, all these statues, all this gaudiness. I hear that lutenist ponce in England's got Holbein on a leash! I'm stuck out in this swamp, middle of nowhere, nothing to show I'm a prince.

ALBERT: Elector.

JOACHIM: Sentenced to this Schloss. Feel the need to fill it with art.

ALBERT: The painter's best chum is Luther.

JOACHIM: I don't care if he's bum chums with Satan.

ALBERT: Entertaining Protestants! Your wife their convert –

JOACHIM: Don't start me on that.

(*JOACHIM'S countenance persuades ALBERT against continuing on this tack.*)

ALBERT: This painter, Cranach. Did a fine job in my Cathedral. Very nice set of Stations to the Cross.

JOACHIM: You sly old hypocrite.

ALBERT: One needs keep an eye on this kind of man.

JOACHIM: I know about keeping eyes.

(*He motions to BENNO, who comes.*)

New man in town. Painter. Lucas Cranach. At the Inn. Tell him you'll assist him with anything.

ALBERT: And keep your eye on him.

JOACHIM: He knows!

(*BENNO leaves.*)

ALBERT: You miss Elizabeth.

JOACHIM: I said never mind about –

ALBERT: Anyone new caught your eye?

JOACHIM: Your business?

ALBERT: I have a responsibility toward the souls of princes of the faith.

JOACHIM: I'm a mere elector.

ALBERT: Make a mistake with the wrong woman, you'll wreck us all.

JOACHIM: Would you like music?

ALBERT: A choir?

JOACHIM: I've minstrels at the Schloss.

ALBERT: Sounds vulgar.

JOACHIM: The boy on the tabor is very pretty.

ALBERT: You've twisted my arm.

(*JOACHIM smiles and claps his hands for the band. Medieval pop songs resound.*)

*

4

(*The Inn. CRANACH is settling into the best room; all ostentatious gentility. He makes a survey of the accommodation with his young son, LUCAS, who shakes and fondles the various objects as they are listed.*)

CRANACH: Item, one bed.

LUCAS: Fine feather eiderdown.

CRANACH: Item, one pillow.

LUCAS: Freshly puffed.

CRANACH: Item, one bedside table.

LUCAS: Nicely carved legs.

(*He lifts a lamp.*)

Plenty of oil.

CRANACH: One Bible.

LUCAS: Latin.

CRANACH: Urgh.

(*LUCAS lets the book drop with a thud.*)

Item, one fire. Best place for that ghastly Bible.

LUCAS: Decent stock of wood. Keep out the chill.

CRANACH: They know how to treat one, provincials.

(*He wanders to the window.*)

Not much of a view. Very flat, Berlin-Cölln. Pretty river. A bit swampy... I hope there's no mosquitoes!

LUCAS: No netting.

(*CRANACH notices something out of the window.*)

CRANACH: What's that?

(*He peers.*)

My goodness…

(*LUCAS comes across to the window.*)

LUCAS: What?

CRANACH: Follow my finger. No, not that! That's a field. There.

LUCAS: What? Oh dear heavens!

CRANACH: I suppose they must keep their villeins in line.

LUCAS: The barbarians haven't hung them in cages.

CRANACH: So behind the times. Brutal.

LUCAS: Merely to guard their inheritance.

CRANACH: One wouldn't mind if they were protecting the earnings from honest labour. From production and distribution of goods.

LUCAS: Making it all add up?

CRANACH: Good lad. These old ways don't add up. That's why they have to be so cruel.

LUCAS: We were rather cruel to our peasants.

CRANACH: Change takes time. Brother Martin recognised that the peasants' little revolt… It wasn't an opportune moment.

LUCAS: Change will come?

CRANACH: As everyone learns to work for their keep. A good living has to be earned.

34

(*A knock on the door.*)

Who's that?

BENNO: (*Off*) Letters for Master Cranach.

CRANACH: Enter.

(*BENNO enters.*)

Put them on the bed.

(*BENNO obeys.*)

Wherever one goes these days one is preceded by the post.

LUCAS: That's why they call it post haste.

CRANACH: Very good.

(*He looks at the letters.*)

All from Wittenberg I presume. All bills? Perhaps we should put ourselves in the post and let the letters take the coach. At least for one single day a respite from the bills.

(*He opens one of the letters. He becomes aware of Benno looking at him.*)

It wasn't just the post was it?

BENNO: My master, the Elector Joachim – we call him Nestor – for he is wise -

CRANACH: And agèd?

BENNO: He still has years in him.

CRANACH: Nightmare billing a corpse.

BENNO: The Elector has put me at your disposal.

CRANACH: I've my own journeyman staying, as you can see.

(*He gestures at LUCAS.*)

LUCAS: Journeyman? Oh really, father!

(*CRANACH hushes LUCAS.*)

BENNO: If there's anything you should need in Berlin...

CRANACH: I'm familiar with the town.

BENNO: The cheapest spots for quality goods.

CRANACH: Let the lad know. As to your spying, let's get the facts out the way. I know Martin Luther. He's godfather to my child. I have no political nor religious affiliations.

(*LUCAS goggles his eyes. CRANACH scowls at him.*)

               I am an Artist. I Serve All Mankind.

BENNO: Should you wish to be served by womankind...

CRANACH: (*To LUCAS*) Don't you enjoy travelling in Papist territories? Everything provided gratis by the Prince. In the Netherlands one has to pop into shops with ready cash.

               (*To BENNO*) Have you travelled?

BENNO: Travel's not for the likes of me.

CRANACH: Not missing much. This coach, that Inn. If it were up to me we'd stay put in Wittenberg. Come here.

(*BENNO comes to the window. CRANACH points.*)

That.

(*He points out of the window.*)

BENNO: The Spree.

CRANACH: That is no spree.

(*BENNO sees what CRANACH is pointing at.*)

LUCAS: Probably payment for too much of a spree.

CRANACH: (*To LUCAS*) So full of cracks today.

(*To BENNO*) Your Elector hang many, does he?

BENNO: As many as offend him.

CRANACH: Getting a bit old fashioned now, letting them simply dangle. Snot icicles froze on a winter nose. Thaw of decomposition. Drops on the road.

LUCAS: Health and safety.

CRANACH: In Saxony, the innovation is to hang them in cages.

LUCAS: Saves a passers-by from falling bits.

BENNO: The condemned starve in these cages?

LUCAS: They're racked and garrotted first.

CRANACH: Their couple of hours caged is merely a daze.

BENNO: Our way, one quick dance in the wind and all's done.

LUCAS: You'd prefer that?

BENNO: I prefer not to offend.

CRANACH: When will the Elector see me?

BENNO: Tomorrow. Anything for tonight?

CRANACH: Point my lad in the direction of the cheapest apothecary. We're bound to need pigments.

BENNO: (*To LUCAS*) I'll be delighted to show you the way.

(*CRANACH shoos LUCAS off; the lad leaves with BENNO. CRANACH flings himself on the bed, tired out.*)

*

5

(*A street in Berlin, near the market. BENNO shows LUCAS up the street; they disappear. AVA enters with GRETEL.*)

GRETEL: Oh my Lord.

AVA: Are you all right?

GRETEL: Come over giddy.

AVA: Why won't you go home?

GRETEL: We've still got onion, apples, flour and salt -

AVA: You're ever so pale.

GRETEL: Meat for supper. Can't have your uncle coming home to empty plate.

AVA: I'll fetch the rest.

GRETEL: Leave you out on your own in the market place? I said was giddy, not silly.

AVA: You're not well.

GRETEL: What do you know of the world?

AVA: Not enough and to tell you the truth it's about time I knew more.

GRETEL: Your father's child.

AVA: I'm of an age –

GRETEL: That's what worries me.

AVA: Maybe I'll run into Dad! Round some corner, duck down some alley, there he is, lost and found.

GRETEL: How many times do I have to tell you? He's gone off.

AVA: Is he milk now?

GRETEL: On business.

AVA: What business? Don't say it's none of mine! These fainting fits of yours have some connection to Dad.

GRETEL: I have found your father's leaving us upsetting.

AVA: He didn't say goodbye.

GRETEL: He's always coming and going.

AVA: When's he coming back?

GRETEL: He offended someone with a lot of power. He has to keep his head down.

AVA: Uncle must have a word with the Elector.

GRETEL: Hush yourself! As if your uncle's word could sway the Elector. He informs the Elector a man has dissed his Lordship, that man within hours is swinging by his neck. Tell him a man's life's worth saving and that man be saved? We can dream. You oughtn't be out in this world of harm. At least be fortressed with your hood up.

(GRETEL pulls AVA'S hood up.)

AVA: Now I feel a right 'nana.

GRETEL: So much like your father. Oh!

(GRETEL staggers, giddy.)

AVA: Get off home! I'll get the last few things and join you in less than half hour.

(GRETEL demurs but then gives AVA the basket and a rosary.)

GRETEL: Twenty minutes. Keep praying to Our Lady and you'll be safe.

AVA: Sense reigns.

(GRETEL hands AVA some coins.)

GRETEL: Mutton for supper. If you can't get that, a plucked chicken.

AVA: Ready the veg. I'll wring the tastiest joint of meat from the butcher.

GRETEL: Don't be flirting with the butcher. Blessed Virgin, keep this girl from the admiration of lewd eyes.

AVA: Go on!

(*GRETEL reluctantly staggers off, AVA watching her go. AVA waits a moment, looks around, lowers her hood. She breathes deep. Up the street, LUCAS enters. He stops, stares at AVA. She looks up the street, notices him. She panics, goes to put her hood up again then suddenly decides against it. LUCAS comes down to her.*)

LUCAS: Miss.

AVA: I haven't the time.

LUCAS: A moment, miss.

AVA: Not from round here, are you?

LUCAS: It's so obvious?

AVA: You don't half speak odd. Nice shirt.

LUCAS: I've felt rather conspicuous in it. Folk in Berlin don't appear to follow the fashions...

AVA: Where you from?

LUCAS: Wittenberg.

AVA: A Proddie?

LUCAS: I'm of the Reformed church, yes.

AVA: Oughtn't be talking with you!

(*She hurries off down the street, fingering her rosary. LUCAS shouts after her*)

LUCAS: Don't run. I want to talk with you. I'd like to paint you!

(*She stops in her tracks. She walks back to him.*)

AVA: Paint me?

LUCAS: What I said.

AVA: Heard it told the Proddies make the best paintings.

LUCAS: Lucas Cranach.

AVA: What's doing stuff for our Elector?

LUCAS: I'm flattered you've heard of me.

AVA: I've a family connection to the court.

LUCAS: Let me paint you.

(*AVA thinks, but not for long. She puts her rosary in the shopping bag.*)

AVA: I know somewhere we can talk without being gossiped of.

LUCAS: Lead me anywhere.

AVA: It's you had better not lead me astray.

(*They walk off down the street together.*)

*

6

(*The enclosed walls of a small cell come down. ALBERT unfolds a rather snazzy small, ornate, portable shrine with an ivory carving. He gets down to his prayers.*)

ALBERT: My Lord, it must seem as if all I ever bring You is my troubles. Oh, You must think – if I dare presume to put words in my Lord's mouth... I haven't been struck down so I'll go on. You say to Your Self, "Oh here he comes again, Bishop moaner, nag in a velvet gown, carping on of dangerous times; what a time I had when I was with men! Accused of blasphemy, despised, rejected; a man of sorrows and acquainted of grief. What grief does he know? Fat and sassy, all frocked up, men at his command and respect laid at his feet!" But my dear Lord, for me these are dangerous times.

(*He crosses himself.*)

My brother. Alone. Sans feminine company. Unlike me, he likes feminine company. Rather too fond. I worry... I don't know why I tell You, You're bound to know, being omnipotent and all. I suppose the point is that I show you that I am conscious of what is happening – I am worried that if he creates a public scandal... Of course, being omnipotent You must be aware that I am conscious of what is happening but perhaps this is – yes that must be it! – this is You allowing me to show You that I see me, even though You already see me seeing, You grant me the time and place to be conscious before You. Oh, You're really very good.

(*He wrings his hands together, fiddles with a rosary.*)

I'm absolutely committed to being set aside for You. We must be special. Yes. Now, I know I like to have a bit of... a... well, You know. But I keep myself away from the things which tend towards the Natural Man. The Old Adam. The serpent. The tree. The woman proffering her body...

(*He genuflects.*)

I do worry about my brother. That cow! Oh, she is though. And now Joachim's – well... all alone with his fists. Spanking them out in vain...

(*He raises his arms to the Lord.*)

Come through the painter. I know You like to come through painters. I don't know why you favour painters so much, the Italian ones especially, they spend all their time gobbling criminals and tinkering with illiterates. The German ones, all they care for is cash on demand. But You do come through them. Much like You do come through us, your clergy. As You do come through me. Joachim won't listen. He hasn't the

44

consolation of boys. You do tend to speak through sods a fair bit, don't You?

(*Wonders if he's gone too far.*)

Just saying.

(*He prays, earnestly.*)

Keep my brother away from thoughts which might lead to him losing grip on the reigns of the state. She left him to become a Godless Protestant!

(*He sniggers.*)

Shouldn't laugh.

(*He peeks at the shrine.*)

Oh come on now, I bet You did. Over those who went down in the flood? A moment or two of Divine schadenfreude.

(*He goes back to praying.*)

I pray the painter paints a picture helps prevent my brother's fall. You can't afford to lose Brandenburg to the Prods. And neither can I.

(*He prays, murmuring feverishly in Latin.*)

*

7

(*The prayers melt into moans of pleasure as the walls fly away, revealing a field. Clothes are strewn on the ground. The sound of a climax, then carefree giggles. AVA and LUCAS emerge naked from behind a tree.*)

LUCAS: Are you sure that was all right?

AVA: Not at all.

(*LUCAS, looks down, ashamed.*)

It was wonderful!

LUCAS: You rascal!

(*They hug and snog, ending up lying on the grass.*)

I wish we could stay here forever.

AVA: We'd soon get hungry. And freeze come the set of sun.

LUCAS: Would it were The Golden Age.

AVA: You what?

LUCAS: The Golden Age. My – I've painted it.

AVA: I can't wait to see your paintings.

LUCAS: I can't wait to paint you.

(*They snog.*)

The Golden Age ended long ago but 'twill come again and come soon. Men and women will frolic. They'll toil not, neither shall they grieve. Enjoying each other's company. Always naked. Eternally carefree.

AVA: The Garden of Eden?

LUCAS: Without the snake and the ban on fruit.

AVA: You Proddies don't half have funny ideas. You believe in this Golden Age?

LUCAS: We must work hard for it.

AVA: People have worked hard since long enough. No Golden Age comes.

LUCAS: Who has the work been for?

AVA: Don't look at me.

LUCAS: Emperors, princes, Papist Bishops.

AVA: The devil's sermon.

LUCAS: Is a better world the devil's plan?

AVA: You speak like my Dad. But he says Proddies are hypocrites. He says your peasants fought for paradise an' got a good kicking.

LUCAS: The peasants wanted too much, too soon. I don't approve what happened to them. It was brutal. Yet the peasants themselves committed terrible atrocities. It's very confusing.

AVA: You're a thoughtful scoundrel, aren't you?

LUCAS: Scoundrel?

AVA: My scoundrel.

LUCAS: That's all right then.

(*They snog.*)

In your Papist lands, each generation walks the round. Trudging in circles. Do like your parents. They did like their parents before them. The world we're bringing... If your parents work hard, they better themselves. Set you up so you can do better. And your kids then do better than you. Each generation improves on the last and, at last, The Golden Age blooms!

AVA: Just like my dad.

LUCAS: Most girls go blank when I speak this way.

AVA: Are they ninnies?

LUCAS: Rich ninnies. My father would have me to marry one.

(*AVA is downcast.*)

No chance of that now.

AVA: Why?

LUCAS: I've met someone who blasts them all to hell. I sow good seed and, in so doing, I sow the Golden Age. I must sow it in the proper ground.

(*AVA looks at him, not quite getting it.*)

You're my garden.

(*She stares at him. The bells ring.*)

AVA: Oh my Lady!

(*She springs up.*)

I have to get home.

(*She grabs her clothes, dresses.*)

LUCAS: I must see you again. The Golden Age depends on it.

AVA: Where you staying?

LUCAS: The Inn at the market square.

AVA: I'll come by tomorrow. If you're not there, I'll wait.

LUCAS: I'll be there. You promise you'll come?

AVA: Cross my heart and hope to –

LUCAS: Never say die.

(*He kisses her. She gazes into his eyes then runs off. LUCAS watches after her, then punches the sky.*)

*

8

(*Walls close in again to the peasant house. BENNO stands looking out of the window, as GRETEL frets on a chair.*)

GRETEL: I don't know what I was thinking.

BENNO: You weren't thinking.

GRETEL: How can I be expected to think? Me son hung -

BENNO: Your favourite son.

GRETEL: You needn't envy a corpse.

BENNO: Someone's grabbed her. To die on the same day as her father, there's a trick of fate.

GRETEL: Your worse than your father. Always trying to conjure the worst into being.

BENNO: Right though, wasn't he? All his fears for my brother have come up flourishing weeds. All of them thrashings for nothing.

GRETEL: It was the thrashings made your brother bad. Bred his resentment.

BENNO: Daddy thrashed me more! Did me the world of good.

GRETEL: Turned you into your father.

BENNO: And who was my brother like? You? Is that why you only had love for him? He neglected that poor girl's care, as you now have.

GRETEL: She probably met a friend –

BENNO: Raped and discarded. Dead in a ditch.

(*GRETEL weeps.*)

It's better for her if she is. If she comes home now,
I'll take a stick and —

GRETEL: Ghost of your father.

(*BENNO glares at her.*)

*

9

(*Walls of the Schloss tower over its chapel's confessional.
ALBERT and JOACHIM linger outside.*)

JOACHIM: Best to get it over and done with.

ALBERT: Entirely.

JOACHIM: You promise not to judge?

ALBERT: Who am I to judge?

JOACHIM: Or laugh?

ALBERT: You need to forget I'm your brother.

JOACHIM: God knows I've tried.

ALBERT: He asks me to behave.

JOACHIM: Sorry.

ALBERT: Get in.

JOACHIM: All right.

(*JOACHIM gets into the confessional, then demurs.*)

If I hear one snigger —

ALBERT: In!

(*JOACHIM gets in. ALBERT raises his eyes to the heavens then get in the other side. He fiddles with the cushion.*)

JOACHIM: In the name of the Father and of the Son and of the —

ALBERT: Hold on. I need to get myself comfy.

JOACHIM: Oh, you settle yourself in for a good old earwig.

(*ALBERT gets comfy.*)

ALBERT: Right.

JOACHIM: Comfortable?

ALBERT: I am.

JOACHIM: In the name of the Father and of the Son and of the Holy Spirit, my last confession was twenty months ago.

ALBERT: Too long.

JOACHIM: I can't confess to any old priest, can I? In my position.

ALBERT: Though the Lord is on high he lives with the low but the proud he knows from afar.

JOACHIM: You what?

ALBERT: What have you been up to?

(*JOACHIM considers if he should dare, then -*)

JOACHIM: Tossing!

(*JOACHIM nods, having suspected as much.*)

>A great tugging – oh my wrist – morning, noon and night. Gallons of wasted seed spilled on the sheets, in the jakes, in the woods. I ride off ahead of my men, jump down, skulk behind the thickest tree, breeches round my knees, looking to see that no one is peeking, spank one out.

ALBERT: I knew it.

JOACHIM: Don't tell me you don't. Oh I forgot, you put it in lads.

ALBERT: This isn't about me. What are your thoughts?

JOACHIM: Thoughts?

ALBERT: When you're…

JOACHIM: Cunt of course. What d'you think, I'm one of your buggers?

ALBERT: Any particular…?

JOACHIM: (*Shrugs*) My wife's from memory.

ALBERT: Conjugal rights do stretch to reminiscence.

JOACHIM: Servant wenches.

ALBERT: Urgh.

JOACHIM: You're not supposed to judge!

ALBERT: It's not you, it's me. I'm such a terrific snob.

JOACHIM: A certain citizen's wife –

ALBERT: What's that?

JOACHIM: He's a local printer.

ALBERT: You haven't been making advances?

JOACHIM: No. Although...

ALBERT: Oh no.

JOACHIM: She is never upset to see me.

ALBERT: You flirt with her?

JOACHIM: I simply say hello and she –

ALBERT: What sort of thoroughbred numbskull are you? A printer! And so he publishes your foul offence? "Hold the press, we've got here a right pamphlet. No to droit du seigneur!" Your shame would find no end.

JOACHIM: I need guidance.

ALBERT: You need penance. You must never see her again.

(*JOACHIM slumps.*)

Do you hear me? Never.

JOACHIM: All right.

ALBERT: On pain of excommunication.

JOACHIM: Bit harsh.

ALBERT: The church does what it has to do to maintain Her dignity. And that of Her representatives. How many Electors now have gone to Luther? If one of the few who remain loyal to the Pope gets caught with his hands in a printer's wife...

JOACHIM: All right! My penance?

ALBERT: You shall lie abed at night in sackcloth and ashes. Under-clothe your body in lice-ridden rags. Plunge your soul in sorrow. Correct your faults by harsh treatment of yourself. Use the plainest meat and drink for the sake of your soul and not of your belly. You shall nourish prayer by fasting whole days and nights in a row. You shall moan and weep and wail to the Lord your God. Cast yourself at the feet of the priests, fall on your knees before those who are dear to the Lord and beseech them to plead for you.

JOACHIM: Well that's me told then.

ALBERT: Now, contrition.

JOACHIM: Oh all right.

(*He sinks to his knees.*)

Oh me old pegs.

ALBERT: Being contrite does not involve complaining about your knees.

JOACHIM: This floor.

ALBERT: Contrite!

JOACHIM: O my God. I am heartily sorry for having offended you and I detest my sins because I dread the loss of heaven and the pains of hell but most of all because I have offended my God, who are all good and deserve all my love. I firmly resolve with the help of your grace to confess my sins, to do penance and to amend my life. Amen.

ALBERT: Give thanks to the Lord for He is good.

JOACHIM: His mercy endures.

(*ALBERT comes out of the confessional. He looks down on his brother, who looks up at him, sheepish and ashamed.*)

ALBERT: Mind you sin no more.

JOACHIM: I am but a man.

ALBERT: With responsibilities!

(*ALBERT leaves. JOACHIM kneels there abject. He gets up, rubs his knees. His hands, almost involuntarily, travel upwards...*)

*

10

(*The walls contract for the Inn. Cranach is in his room, going through accounts in ledgers. He adds, subtracts, crosses out, writes in. Occasionally he exclaims excitedly, or in frustration. A knock on the door.*)

CRANACH: Come.

(*Lucas enters tentatively.*)

Don't stand there lingering like an apprentice at the threshold a brothel.

(*Lucas comes in.*)

How did you like your walk about Berlin-Cölln? Very cold, isn't it?

LUCAS: It's simply the best place I've ever been!

(*Cranach is taken aback.*)

CRANACH: What will you be like in Florence?

LUCAS: What a world there is beyond Wittenberg.

CRANACH: Get your mind on business. I think we can persuade these puppets of popery to spend money on our goods. Goods being the only good -

LUCAS: The town really has its attractions.

CRANACH: What are the only good?

LUCAS: Eh?

CRANACH: Do you listen to anything I say?

LUCAS: I –

CRANACH: What are the only good?

LUCAS: Goods.

CRANACH: Selling frees us.

LUCAS: What will the Elector buy?

CRANACH: He'll want his portrait done. I've painted him before, long ago. Suppose he's got fatter. We've all got fatter. You'll get fat someday.

God's sign of industry, fat. Yet the Elector is fat
because... Hold on!

(*Cranach goes to the door, looks out. Shuts it. Comes back in to Lucas.*)

He inherited his fatness. Obesity you could say
came with his territory. Look –

(*Cranach picks up the ledger, opens it. Lucas looks at the page.*)

Outgoings last month four hundred and seven
gulden and four groschen. Incomings last month
three hundred and fifty-six gulden and seven
groschen. The world must make sense. I've
overextended us on the mortgage. We're
employing too many master painters. Use more
outworkers. We can get them for less than -

LUCAS: One gulden and nine groschen.

CRANACH: Don't be silly we pay them more than that.

LUCAS: That's what you give me.

(*Cranach closes the ledger.*)

CRANACH: That's what you're worth.

LUCAS: It might be handy to have more money.

CRANACH: I'm telling him we're in debt and he asks for more
money! Why do you need money? You'll only
spend it on shirts and you've enough of them.

LUCAS: I might not want to spend it on myself.

CRANACH: Who else will you spend on? A friend? One that can't pay his own way? That's a parasite.

LUCAS: My friends all pay their own way.

CRANACH: I don't like Schnibber's son.

LUCAS: Erich always buys his round. Why don't you like him?

CRANACH: He talks like a girl. "Knowest thou that the effeminate shall not, etcetera, etcetera." It's him that drags you shirt shopping. You've got into debt, haven't you? Is it Jews?

LUCAS: It's not myself. It's not my friends. It's not Jews.

CRANACH: It's a woman. Of course! He's old enough for women. Why didn't I notice? Listen, when I was your age... Oh, I hate speaking of this with the kids but I told Hans so I'd better tell you. At your age what you want from a woman can be bought for a groschen or less.

LUCAS: Men buy gifts for the women they love.

CRANACH: What do you know about love? You've met someone here?

(*Lucas nods.*)

That's why he's keen on Berlin! Who is she?

LUCAS: Local girl.

CRANACH: Papist?

LUCAS: Aren't they all?

CRANACH: Who are her people?

LUCAS: I've no idea.

CRANACH: A burgher's daughter can bring a decent dower.

LUCAS: I don't care who her people are.

CRANACH: Are you demented?

LUCAS: I don't think they're anything much.

(*CRANACH stares.*)

From the way she speaks and dresses they're clearly just... ordinary folk.

CRANACH: Do you mean shopkeepers?

LUCAS: I shouldn't suppose they're anything like that. Service or carriers or –

CRANACH: Peasants!

LUCAS: I refuse to use that word to describe her. She won't be a peasant once we're married. She'll be a respectable lady.

CRANACH: A peasant! Where did you find her?

LUCAS: On the street.

CRANACH: That's where they tend to be found in the towns. Find them on the street. Take them down an alley. "Up he goes and shoots his gifts and washes

once he's down-o!" Don't give them your name
lest gifts get baked as a bun.

(*LUCAS is staring at him agog.*)

What?

LUCAS: I can't believe what I'm hearing.

CRANACH: It's about time we had this sort of chat. You can't
stay a child forever.

LUCAS: All these paintings we churn out on religious and
moral themes -

CRANACH: Now you're being silly.

LUCAS: - your advice is that I abandon milkmaids after a
quick one up the alley?

CRANACH: She's a milkmaid?

LUCAS: No! I don't know.

CRANACH: Gets worse.

LUCAS: Rank hypocrisy.

CRANACH: What are the paintings?

LUCAS: I said, rank –

CRANACH: What are they?

(*He bangs the ledger on Lucas' head.*)

LUCAS: Ow! Goods.

(*Cranach slams the ledger down.*)

I thought my father's art was more than that.

(*Lucas goes to walks out, Cranach grabs his arm.*)

CRANACH: You think that Grünewald's any different? You think Durer doesn't come down to cash? How do you think he affords the hairdos? Doesn't mean the gift's not God's. Money's the signature of God!

(*LUCAS wrestles himself from his father's arms and exits. Cranach stands in the doorway, fuming. In frustration he bangs on the wall.*)

*

11

(*The sound of the last few swipes of a violent lashing accompany the walls closing to accommodate the peasant home. In her room, AVA kneels with her back exposed, red stripes on it. BENNO stands over her, holding a thin branch. GRETEL stands, shaking, in the doorway.*)

BENNO: Worrying your grandmother like that.

GRETEL: This has hardly alleviated my anxiety.

BENNO: It's helped with mine.

(*AVA attempts to rise. She staggers, falls back to her knees.*)

AVA: Don't you go thinking I'll stand for much of this.

(*She tries to cover her back but it smarts. GRETEL goes to her.*)

GRETEL: Let the air soothe it a while. You'll probably have to sleep on your stomach tonight.

AVA: (*To BENNO*) You don't have any right!

GRETEL: I'd to say that to your grandfather until I was
               blue in the face. But his house, his rules...

AVA: This is as much my father's house.

GRETEL: I'll get you a balm.

(*GRETEL hurries from the room.*)

AVA: I won't live in your house.

BENNO: What other house will have you? We can guess.
               Is that what you want for yourself?

AVA: Do I want this?

(*She squirms in pain.*)

BENNO: Your father wouldn't accept Dad's whipping
               neither. Some horses won't. Proud beasts but
               sooner or later they're left raggedy grazing on
               marshland or in a bowl, food for hunting hounds.

(*GRETEL re-enters with a balm.*)

AVA: Dad said you'd turn out just like grandpa.

BENNO: That's not fair.

GRETEL: It's not altogether unfair, to be fair.

(*GRETEL begins applying the balm. AVA's lines are punctuated
with her gasps in pain.*)

AVA: You accept things. A man who accepts things will
               sooner or later do them.

BENNO: I don't accept you royally buggering up your life.

GRETEL: Mind your language.

BENNO: You come home all hours, sooner or later –

AVA: There's a whole wide world out there!

BENNO: Do you know what kind of a world it is?

AVA: I like meeting new folk.

GRETEL: Your uncle's concerned that you'll get yourself in trouble. Your father got your mother into trouble. It was the death of her.

AVA: Neither of you think I should've been born.

(*They don't answer.*)

BENNO: That your birth killed your mother can't be denied.

AVA: Thank you.

GRETEL: Fragile little thing. She was fourteen. Your father was much to blame.

AVA: Where is Dad? If he were here –

BENNO: He isn't.

AVA: - he'd break your ugly face.

BENNO: I haven't the energy to beat you again.

(*BENNO goes out. AVA goes to the bed, lays down. On her back it's agony. She cries and turns onto her side.*)

AVA: I won't forgive him this.

GRETEL: He'd wouldn't forgive himself if he didn't. Don't be late home again.

(*AVA unthinkingly rolls onto her back. She screams in agony, sits upright.*)

AVA: There is a better world out there, fresh faced and noble.

GRETEL: Oh my Ava. If you've an idea some handsome young fellow will sweep you away, take it from me – in all the world, there ain't no such bloke. Better pray.

(*AVA closes her eyes tight and moves her lips. GRETEL continues to minister to AVA's back.*)

*

12

(*Walls expand to accommodate the hall of the Schloss. JOACHIM, wearing sackcloth, greets CRANACH.*)

JOACHIM: Master Cranach! Excellent to see you.

CRANACH: It's been too long.

JOACHIM: We've both put on weight.

CRANACH: God's proof to the world He's blessed us.

JOACHIM: You're staring at my garments?

CRANACH: Your own affair.

JOACHIM: Penance. I owe one or two apologies to our Lord.

CRANACH: That does you credit.

JOACHIM: Does it? How is your friend Brother Martin?

CRANACH: Hale and hearty.

JOACHIM: The schism should never have been.

CRANACH: Alas –

JOACHIM: Communities, friendships, families torn on its bull's horn.

CRANACH: The consequences have been unfortunate –

JOACHIM: For some of us more than others.

CRANACH: Belief is –

(*CRANACH pauses; JOACHIM is glaring at him.*)

JOACHIM: Go on.

CRANACH: Belief is a personal thing.

JOACHIM: Ah now that's where you're wrong.

CRANACH: Perhaps if I lived in this neck of the woods I should believe otherwise.

JOACHIM: Not a man of conviction then?

CRANACH: A man of business.

JOACHIM: At least you're honest.

CRANACH: Art.

JOACHIM: Craft.

CRANACH: Such a long time since I painted your Excellency.

JOACHIM: Had less chops then. I'm proud of these chops. My taste in clothes has improved too, shame you had to catch me like this.

CRANACH: I'm sure as a rule you look absolutely smashing.

JOACHIM: My brother would say these garments suit me best. I bought a tailor back from Italy. Stole him from a Medici. You artisans are all alike, whoever pays you best. Have you travelled in Italy?

CRANACH: Once to see the Masters.

JOACHIM: They do flesh very well, don't you think?

CRANACH: And this perspective thing. A new portrait shall we say?

JOACHIM: You're accompanied by your son?

CRANACH: I am.

JOACHIM: Good boy?

CRANACH: A funny age.

JOACHIM: Tell me about it. I worry mine might follow his mother from Rome. I suppose you'd like that.

CRANACH: I've never painted young Joachim. I'll tell you what, we do one of you, one of your son. You could hang them next to each other. Joachim Two and Joachim One.

JOACHIM: Two for the price of one eh?

CRANACH: Buy one, get one half price.

JOACHIM: Done!

(*They shake on it.*)

It's difficult, this Dad stuff. Trying to pass on your values. Your son...

CRANACH: Lucas.

(*JOACHIM nods.*)

JOACHIM: We try our best to make ourselves a little doppelganger. Then they go and develop some silly little mind of their own. What's wrong with my mind? What's wrong with yours? Apart from you're a Prod but let's face it we're good at what we do. Joachim must fill my boots. Lucas yours as well, I'm guessing?

CRANACH: (*Nods*) He paints.

JOACHIM: Why change a method that works? I made mine sign a contract. You'll like this. Proddies love contracts. That's why you flock to that puppet play about the doctor who signs with the devil. What's his name?

CRANACH: Faust.

JOACHIM: Joachim won't inherit a drop if he strays from Rome. His mother strayed. She can rot in that pokey old manor at Wittenberg. To hell with your mate Luther! Power and property kids want more than their own little ways. Does the younger Lucas want his own little way?

CRANACH: He wants to marry a peasant.

JOACHIM: Sod that for a game of soldiers! Mind you, I could've told you that's where your Proddie pull-down-the-Church bollocks would lead.

CRANACH: He'll learn the error of his ways.

JOACHIM: Break 'em to make 'em.

(*ALBERT appears at the door.*)

Oh do come in brother!

(*ALBERT enters the room.*)

Our Dad had to break Alby here. Didn't always want the Church, did you?

ALBERT: Don't rake it all up.

JOACHIM: In the end he saw sense. Once he realised I wasn't going to keel over or get myself killed. Quite like the dresses though, don't you?

ALBERT: Master Cranach, are you recovered from our bone-rattling ride?

CRANACH: The bed in the Inn is soft and downy. A good night's sleep has soothed my aches.

ALBERT: The bed my brother has given me is stiff as old boards.

JOACHIM: You're too pampered in your Bishop's palace, Alby.

ALBERT: My brother sleeps in a bed of fleece and swan's down. Sleeps alone. What will you paint for my brother?

CRANACH: We've been talking about a portrait.

JOACHIM: Two portraits. Time young Joachim had his picture done.

ALBERT: All is vanity.

JOACHIM: Rehearsing a sermon?

ALBERT: These are the only commissions?

CRANACH: I'm happy to do whatever the Elector requires.

ALBERT: He also requires –

JOACHIM: I think I can speak for myself –

ALBERT: In fact the situation necessitates that he –

JOACHIM: I am still here you know.

ALBERT: - have some moral representation to contemplate.

JOACHIM: That's right, spend my money for me. It's not enough he spends Rome's.

ALBERT: A painted cloth must keep him in awe or else he'll sell eternity for a toy. He toys with himself. His fists are his only bedfellows.

JOACHIM: Is this appropriate?

ALBERT: If talk of the moral issues with which you wrestle is not appropriate with your confessor and your court artist –

JOACHIM: The moral issues with which I wrestle?

ALBERT: (*To CRANACH*) You offer emblematic scenes from ethical fables?

CRANACH: A popular line.

ALBERT: My brother's in a pickle. Marinated in sheets stained with the outcome of his vinegar strokes. Such is life without a wife.

JOACHIM: You'd know about that.

ALBERT: Rome is my betrothed.

(*To CRANACH*) Yes I know you and your friends would say she's my harlot but that's not polite is it? Why are reformers so free with abuse? Abuse and cawing. No doubt you and your friend Martin can't-cack – I hear he has terrible bowels – have giggled and whinnied over my brother's marital tribulation. Instead of this cawing –

CRANACH: I can assure you –

ALBERT: - try to help. Give him a scene to remind him of the temptations of the flesh. Not merely addressed to him as an individual – sad as I should be to contemplate my own flesh and blood baking and broiling in perdition, devils pinching his flesh and one with a beak for a nose screaming in his face "hah-hah-hee" – but something to reinforce the State. A tale that warns princes to tread a proper path. He is not a prince but –

JOACHIM: I elect princes.

CRANACH: The Judgement of Paris. Misjudgement as 'twas. Offered Athena and Hera but – rejecting wisdom and marriage – the nitwit selected Aphrodite. Mere sensual love. As imprudent a choice as there ever was. Leading to war. Siege. Thousands of unnecessary deaths.

JOACHIM: Paris was a very handsome prince.

ALBERT: It's too far removed from reality. Pagan goddesses? For goodness sake. Save the choice of the foolish Trojan for when lovely little Joachim's Elector, unmarried and practising his own whackings of a night.

CRANACH: David! Up on the roof taking the air. What does he see? Bathsheba bathing.

JOACHIM: Bathsheba bathing sounds good.

CRANACH: God's favourite, the greatest of kings but temptation led him to kill her husband, a faithful soldier. I could work in my lord archbishop as the prophet Samuel, scolding his folly.

JOACHIM: Tit naked.

ALBERT: What comeuppance had David? Uriah got buried. Bathsheba was queen. David's son by Bathsheba inherited the throne. We don't want to mess up the line of succession. Think of poor little Joachim.

JOACHIM: I like the idea of Bathsheba's bath!

ALBERT: What we want is –

JOACHIM: I do love this "we".

ALBERT: What my brother requires is a tale where the state is pulled into disarray by princely philandering. Where he gets his just deserts for following his filthy old rampant lusts.

CRANACH: Let me think. There's… No that won't quite do. OR… Almost but not really. Yes! You're going to adore this.

ALBERT: Go on.

CRANACH: I don't see how you could fail to approve.

ALBERT: I'm on the edge of my throne.

JOACHIM: Don't cack.

ALBERT: Shush!

CRANACH: A luscious young woman.

JOACHIM: My interest is perked.

CRANACH: A lustful lord.

ALBERT: Fat in his lust.

JOACHIM: Oi!

CRANACH: A roving eye. A rape. The riot which follows deposes the prince.

ALBERT: Ideal.

CRANACH: Lucrece.

ALBERT: Oh yes.

CRANACH: King Tarquinius too bold.

ALBERT: No pagan gods mixed up in it?

CRANACH: (*Shakes his head*) Only Virtue's ruin justly penalized.

ALBERT: Sold!

JOACHIM: Hold on, it's my money.

CRANACH: Lucrece is painted nude, after her ravishment.

JOACHIM: Is that right?

CRANACH: One look in her eyes tells us how she has been wronged.

ALBERT: Brother, I advise you to –

JOACHIM: Oh all right. How much?

CRANACH: Such a painting would usually cost say one hundred gulden.

JOACHIM: Bit pricey innit?

CRANACH: I'll tell you what, I'll do you a sketch.

ALBERT: Let the dog see the rabbit.

JOACHIM: Bring it to me tomorrow, I'll say if I want.

ALBERT: You should want it, brother.

JOACHIM: I'm the collector and connoisseur and it's for my moral improvement. Tomorrow morning Master Cranach?

(*CRANACH bows.*)

I anticipate a treat.

(*JOACHIM exits.*)

ALBERT: All this talk of nude women and their tits, off for a wank I expect. Tortures of the single life.

CRANACH: Which you'd know all about?

ALBERT: How like your ex-monk friend to stir things up. Down goes history, tradition, doctrine so as he can stick it up a nun.

CRANACH: Priests are not always celibate.

ALBERT: The church is capable of dealing with infringements.

CRANACH: Martin did not reckon so.

ALBERT: When will you come to Mainz and paint me again? I adore the one of me as Saint Jerome. Lovely shade of red. Very vibrant. I am so – I cannot tell you – so relieved we got you to do our Stations of the Cross. 'Twas a toss-up between you and Grünewald. His altarpiece at Isenheim! Christ glows as he leaps from the tomb but the crucifixion itself. The skin of Christ. Dead. He did die, there's no denying. But. The flesh. Torn. Ripped. Shredded. Our Lord was flogged a fair bit. But. Horrid thorns sticking out of his skin. Oh, it's realistic. No need to convince me of that. Skin pallid. Beginning to rot. I know it was probably a baking hot day but it's not what you want on your wall. The monks at Isenheim might like it. They're good monks, not like your mate. Pilgrims coming to the Cathedral don't want anything so... in-yer-face. Your work always shows such restraint. Do me again. In my study. Add in a lion again. Swathe me once in that beautiful striking shocking red. I wish I could get my tailors to make robes so ruddy. How do you do it?

CRANACH: I've the monopoly on vermillion in Wittenberg.

ALBERT: You crafty Reformer. What if someone were to protest your monopoly like Luther protested Rome's?

CRANACH: You saw what our peasants got.

(*ALBERT smiles.*)

ALBERT: Things settle down again. Your lot have your lands, we have ours. It won't be good for any of us if Brandenburg becomes unstable. Will Lucrece be pretty?

CRANACH: Very.

ALBERT: The consequences of tampering clear?

76

CRANACH: To the discerning viewer.

ALBERT: You're a subtle chap. Don't be too subtle. Your stations. The men harrying Our Lord carrying the cross. Their bums...

CRANACH: I remember being pleased with their bums.

ALBERT: A person who was into bums could be tempted -

CRANACH: You think?

ALBERT: If it weren't for their faces. Such grizzly mugs!

CRANACH: I enjoy painting an ugly phiz.

ALBERT: The Lord giveth and taketh away.

(*CRANACH smiles.*)

This moment between the giving and the taking... It opens a space.

CRANACH: Yes?

ALBERT: Watch this space.

(*CRANACH nods.*)

*

13

(*The walls contain LUCAS's room at the Inn. The door is opened and AVA, hooded, ducks in. LUCAS follows, shutting the door behind them. AVA throws off her hood, laughing.*)

AVA: Sneaking around is fun.

LUCAS: Bit of incognito.

AVA: In what?

LUCAS: Where d'you think I want to get in?

AVA: You're obsessed.

LUCAS: Terrible thing is, I am.

AVA: What's so terrible?

LUCAS: You're a terrible attraction. Terrible as a wild flower shouting how special it is over a field of corn. Awful as the midsummer sun roaring over a hill. As dreadfully dazzling as that sun when it reaches its zenith.

AVA: If you use your brush as good as your mouth -

LUCAS: You know how I use my brush.

(*AVA laughs. They kiss passionately.*)

LUCAS: These are definitely the best moments of my life so far. If I have more such moments, what a life I have to look forwards to! Thank you. And thank You God! I'll spend extra hours on my knees this Sunday.

AVA: God approves of what we do?

LUCAS: God rewards good and punishes wickedness. This feels a lot like reward.

AVA: You Proddies! God's merry old Saint Nicholas to you.

(*LUCAS walks to her, kisses her, caresses her. She kisses him back. His hands stray all over her body. When he reaches her back, she tenses. He looks at her, upset.*)

LUCAS: What's the matter?

AVA: I have some boils on my back.

LUCAS: Let me see.

AVA: They're ugly.

LUCAS: Nothing about you could ever be ugly to me.

(*He tries to pull down her dress. She tries to stop him. He tries harder. She struggles – it's a game for him but deadly serious for her. At last, he pulls off her dress. As he does so, she has her back to him. Her back is covered in welts. He freezes.*)

LUCAS: What is this?

(*AVA tenses. LUCAS spins her around.*)

                Who did it?

AVA: Doesn't matter.

(*She pulls her dress up, covering herself.*)

LUCAS: It matters to me! Whoever it was, I can assure you of one thing: this is the last week, no, the last day, no, the last few hours they shall live.

(*AVA breaks away from him.*)

AVA: Calm yourself.

LUCAS: Horrible.

AVA: He did it because he cares for me.

LUCAS: Strange kind of care.

AVA: When we went walking yesterday... Time flew.

LUCAS: Time out of time.

AVA: Time didn't stop though, did it? I was home late. They worried.

LUCAS: Who are "they"?

AVA: Grandma and uncle. My Dad is... I don't know where he is. Uncle's the only bloke I have looking out for me now.

LUCAS: The only bloke?

AVA: Perhaps there's another.

LUCAS: I would never...

AVA: Your father didn't whip you?

LUCAS: My buttocks were strapped but this! My father is strict but not a brute. My father is –

(*CRANACH bursts into the room in a tizz.*)

CRANACH: He wants Lucrece.

(*He stops, seeing LUCAS with AVA.*)

LUCAS: This is my father.

(*AVA clutches her dress to herself at the same time as nodding. LUCAS turns to CRANACH.*)

This is —

CRANACH: Your peasant love.

(*He turns to AVA.*)

Let your dress fall.

LUCAS: Father!

CRANACH: Let it fall!

(*AVA stares at CRANACH.*)

AVA: When I agreed to take my off clothes for your son, I didn't mean the favour to extend to his entire family.

CRANACH: Your Elector wants Lucrece.

AVA: What's that when it's at home?

CRANACH: (*Alternatively to LUCAS and AVA*) I'd thought he might want... She's a Roman lady... Eve or maybe Venus, they're both very popular... A very virtuous lady... I pitched him Bathsheba, the Judgment of Paris... A terrible thing was done to her... Of course, I've done Lucrece but I don't carry the sketches... Raped... I could try to bash one out from memory but... She killed herself... It's better when there's a model... Pose for me.

(*AVA stares at CRANACH.*)

LUCAS: I am planning on painting this young lady.

AVA: I promised your son —

CRANACH: Do you know who I am?

AVA: His dad, obvious —

CRANACH: I'm Lucas Cranach.

AVA: But —

CRANACH: What?

AVA: He is —

CRANACH: Lucas Cranach?

AVA: So he said.

LUCAS: I am!

CRANACH: He is.

AVA: The famous painter.

CRANACH: No.

AVA: I'm getting lost.

(*CRANACH goes to LUCAS, puts his arm around him.*)

CRANACH: Got the same name as his dad, my son.

(*AVA shoots a look at LUCAS.*)

LUCAS: I have done painting.

CRANACH: He's an apprentice. No doubt he shall be famous, he's not bad and let's face it he's got a leg up. Pose for me.

AVA: You'll pay?

CRANACH: For you naked? Oh yes, and more than he'll pay.

LUCAS: Dad!

AVA: How much?

LUCAS: This is something... me and her... will have to discuss.

CRANACH: Have a good old discuss.

(*CRANACH bows to AVA and goes out.*)

LUCAS: Of course you won't.

AVA: Of course I won't.

LUCAS: Another man see you naked?

AVA: He is your Dad.

LUCAS: Not sure that makes it better.

AVA: He'll pay me.

LUCAS: You don't need money. What's mine is yours.

AVA: He's gonna let you marry me?

LUCAS: Of course.

AVA: He called me "peasant".

LUCAS: He'll come round.

AVA: And how might we get him to come round?

LUCAS: Once he gets to know you, he'll see why I adore you and –

AVA: Can you think of a better way for him to get to know me?

(*LUCAS stares at her.*)

*

14

(*A corridor in the Inn. BENNO and GRETEL are lurking; GRETEL is peeking through the keyhole.*)

BENNO: That's her game. Not satisfied with showing herself off to the young fellow –

GRETEL: I can understand, nice looking young bloke.

BENNO: Now she strips off for the old one. Shameless whore! A fool's errand, respectability. Serve one's master. Do God's commandments. Obey the law. Family drags you in the dirt! Damn my thieving lying braggart brother. Damn you for breeding him. Damn him for breeding a doxy daughter.

(*BENNO shoves GRETEL out of the way, peeks through the keyhole himself.*)

GRETEL: It could be worse.

BENNO: How?

GRETEL: The girl's not an idiot. I am. I married your father. Your father was no scholar. As for you! Your brother, mind, had a brain.

(*BENNO rises from the keyhole.*)

BENNO: Your pride and joy. Hung on the brigand's tree but nevertheless, such a clever-clogs.

GRETEL: Come away home.

BENNO: And leave her?

GRETEL: She's doing well for herself. They'll give her coins for this.

BENNO: What else does she throw in to the bargain?

GRETEL: She can confess. Home!

BENNO: It's my job to keep an eye on this Proddie bastard.

(*BENNO bends to a keyhole again.*)

GRETEL: He calls her corrupt. One glimpse was quite enough for me but oh no, he must keep his eye all pressed -

BENNO: (*At what he sees*) Disgusting!

GRETEL: You know where I'll be.

(*Exit GRETEL. BENNO remains glued to the keyhole, breathing heavily.*)

15

(*In CRANACH'S room. AVA stands naked and posed holding a sword towards her heart as CRANACH sketches her. LUCAS stands to the side, glowering.*)

AVA: But why did this...

CRANACH: Lucrece.

AVA: Why'd she top herself?

CRANACH: It was her only means to prove she'd been ravished.

AVA: She could have just said.

CRANACH: Her ravisher was a powerful man. Her word against his. He simply had to say she'd agreed to bed him –

AVA: Her husband would believe that?

CRANACH: He might distrust.

AVA: He can't have thought much of her. You wouldn't believe that of me, would you Lucas?

LUCAS: Oh no. You'd only pose naked for my father.

(*CRANACH shoots LUCAS a look. AVA, concerned, breaks her pose and moves towards LUCAS.*)

CRANACH: Get back to your pose!

(*AVA reluctantly obeys.*)

It didn't matter whether he believed her or not.
Others might believe her rapist.

AVA: If her husband believes her –

CRANACH: Others might whisper her husband a cuckold.
Make horn signs behind his head and laugh
behind his back.

LUCAS: Know how he feels.

(*Again AVA breaks the pose.*)

CRANACH: Life model is a respectable occupation.

(*To AVA*) Have no worries on that account, my
dear. Back in your pose.

(*AVA does so, CRANACH sketches but then –*)

AVA: How did killing herself make it better?

(*CRANACH flings down his pen in frustration.*)

CRANACH: Lord give me strength! All would know that she
was in earnest. Proof positive of her guiltlessness.
A washing away of the stain.

AVA: Is it not be better to live stained?

LUCAS: What an extraordinary question!

CRANACH: Public opinion does not reckon so.

AVA: I'd rather live with bad opinion than be dead.

CRANACH: Dead you'd be amongst angels.

AVA: I got my angel here and now.

(She gazes at LUCAS.)

LUCAS: She so loved her husband she would die for him.

AVA: Is that how I ought I love you?

LUCAS: Do you love me?

AVA: I have to keep on saying it?

LUCAS: I'm always happy to say it to you.

CRANACH: Youth adores to speak lovey-dovey.

LUCAS: I mean it when I say it.

AVA: I don't?

CRANACH: Does my son say – "Your breasts, like ivory globes I'd travel with my lips which, as unshod feet on a pilgrimage, would circle them round, each kiss a step upon the path to paradise."

AVA: That's gorgeous.

LUCAS: For goodness sake, Father.

CRANACH: Or how about – "Your midriff is formed like a viol de gamba and if my hands could play thereon, they'd move as if over harp strings but the greatest note would be sounded as they hit that rosebud in thy midst."

(AVA giggles, getting off on this. LUCAS is appalled.)

Or says he – "Your thighs are like two columns close composed and if at the weary close of each

day's tedious labour, I could rest my head
between them, the luckiest traveller should I be."

(*AVA has broken her pose; the sword is drooping.*)

LUCAS: Put your hand up, it's like you're pointing the
sword at your...

AVA: Oh!

(*She giggles, gets back in the pose again. CRANACH sketches.*)

What might he describe that as?

CRANACH: What as?

(*AVA nods to where the sword had dropped.*)

Oh, that.

LUCAS: This is intolerable.

CRANACH: You like pretty words don't you, Ava?

AVA: Very much.

CRANACH: Pretty words are sweet keys, they unlock things.
Especially lady's things. Keep your things in a
strong box. To be unlocked by an honest man's "I
will."

LUCAS: I shall marry her.

CRANACH: Pretty, naïve children.

(*He sketches.*)

AVA: Can I see it?

CRANACH: When it's done.

AVA: Will people recognise me?

CRANACH: I don't suppose.

AVA: Why not?

CRANACH: I'll make the face generic.

AVA: You what?

CRANACH: Lucrece is Everywoman.

AVA: You said you needed someone with a figure like mine to pose –

CRANACH: Lucrece possesses a certain shape...

AVA: My shape?

CRANACH: As to the face... I give all my women a similar face. De-individualize to universalize.

AVA: Over my head.

LUCAS: I'll explain it later.

AVA: We've better things to do later.

(*LUCAS blushes. CRANACH raises his eyebrows.*)

I hope some of me comes.

CRANACH: Do you?

AVA: I wouldn't half love being recognised as "that woman from the painting."

CRANACH: I know a lady in Italy… You've heard of Italy?

AVA: Where the Pope is?

LUCAS: Others are there as well.

(*AVA pokes her tongue out at LUCAS.*)

CRANACH: A famous artist in Italy painted the wife of a silk merchant. So he captured her elusive beauty –

AVA: Pretty was she?

CRANACH: More than. A smile any man would swoon to see and dream in that swoon of kissing but never on waking knowing whether that smile said yay or nay. Her painting has become famous. Men see the model and recognise her. They eat her with their eyes. Proposition her. Adorations and obscenities. Many crowd her as she goes to market or Mass. Jackals stalk her. All say they know her. It's only her image they know.

AVA: What's happened to her?

CRANACH: Her smile is one of sadness now. It wistfully tells of her difference now. Eternally set apart from others. Behind glass.

LUCAS: Is that what Ava wants?

(*AVA looks at him, vacantly. She has let the sword slip so that it is pointing at her sex again.*)

Ava!

AVA: What?

LUCAS: Watch yourself.

CRANACH: You're putting her off.

LUCAS: Me?

CRANACH: Outside.

LUCAS: Not bloody likely.

CRANACH: Not a request.

(*LUCAS stares at his father. CRANACH stares his son down.*)

LUCAS: I'll be... just... outside.

(*LUCAS opens the door. BENNO falls in.*)

AVA: OH!

(*AVA covers herself.*)

LUCAS: What the devil?

BENNO: There was a thimble. I was bending to snatch it up.

(*LUCAS grabs BENNO by the scruff of the neck.*)

LUCAS: A peeping Tom!

CRANACH: Deal with him in the corridor, please!

(*He pushes them both out and slams the door. LUCAS and BENNO continue to argue outside. CRANACH turns again to AVA.*)

Back to your pose.

AVA: Not too sure 'bout being alone with you.

CRANACH: It is my son that loves you.

(*BENNO cries off-stage.*)

BENNO: Ow!

AVA: You gonna let him marry me?

CRANACH: Ava, you're dear child. Don't think I fail to see your charms. A father has much to think upon. Pose.

(*AVA smiles uneasily, uncovers again and gets back into the pose. CRANACH sketches.*)

*

16

(*BENNO, with a black eye, ushers CRANACH into a room in the castle. CRANACH clutches his sketchbook.*)

BENNO: The Elector will be with you shortly.

CRANACH: Thank you.

(*CRANACH waits. BENNO hovers.*)

BENNO: All going well?

CRANACH: Very well.

BENNO: Got what you need?

CRANACH: All.

BENNO: Easy to pick up owt in Berlin. On the cheap.

(*CRANACH stares at him.*)

I don't know where we're headed, I really don't.

CRANACH: The future can be hard to scry.

BENNO: Everything's for buying or selling in Proddie lands.

CRANACH: The market —

BENNO: Clothing. Foodstuffs. Building materials. Jewels. Art works. Human flesh.

CRANACH: I wouldn't go so far as —

BENNO: Or is Berlin is ahead of you? In the flesh trade.

CRANACH: Are we talking about yesterday evening? I'm sorry my son gave you that shiner. I've had a word with him.

(*ALBERT enters.*)

ALBERT: There you are.

CRANACH: Your grace.

ALBERT: (*To BENNO*) Sling your hook.

(*BENNO bows and leaves.*)

Someone's thumped him. I'm not surprised. His face offends.

CRANACH: He's screwy.

ALBERT: The sketch. Is it done?

(*CRANACH waves his sketchbook.*)

The Elector has pressing need of moral direction.

CRANACH: He'll get it from this.

ALBERT: Let me gander.

(*CRANACH goes to show ALBERT his sketches but JOACHIM speeds in, back in his luxurious gown and coat.*)

JOACHIM: Keep your mitts off.

ALBERT: Just wanted a peak.

JOACHIM: I'm paying, bags first look.

(*To CRANACH*) Show.

CRANACH: It's only a sketch. The finished item will be more —

ALBERT: Finished?

JOACHIM: Come on, give. You were ready to show the old bollocks here without this kerfuffle.

ALBERT: Why have you abandoned penitential dress?

JOACHIM: You didn't say how long.

ALBERT: I said days and nights in a row.

JOACHIM: That's the fasting. I'm still fasting. In Saxony they hear my belly rumbling. That's enough penance without being dressed up like a twat.

(*To CRANACH*) Show me.

(*CRANACH whips open the sketchbook.*)

CRANACH: Lucrece.

(*JOACHIM looks. He stares. He is transfixed. ALBERT peers over his shoulder; JOACHIM elbows him back.*)

ALBERT: Ow!

(*JOACHIM takes the book, wanders aside with it.*)

Why can't I see?

(*JOACHIM stares at the sketch.*)

CRANACH: You like?

JOACHIM: (*To ALBERT*) Brother, leave us alone.

ALBERT: I like judging art. It's one of my favourite things.

JOACHIM: Carry your lard-arse out before I kick it out.

ALBERT: There's no need for –

JOACHIM: Out!

(*ALBERT wavers.*)

ALBERT: The church expects a full report.

(*JOACHIM is immovable. ALBERT leaves in a huff. JOACHIM goes to the door, closes it. Comes back into the room.*)

CRANACH: Do you like?

(*JOACHIM thinks a moment.*)

JOACHIM: Not much of a face…

CRANACH: Generic. All of my faces tend to... Don't get hung up on the face.

JOACHIM: The curve of the hip.

CRANACH: Very effective. Though I say so myself...

JOACHIM: Effective, he says. It's had an effect on me. You're some damned artist. Who is she?

CRANACH: She?

JOACHIM: The cat's mother. The model, you twot-faced goon.

CRANACH: I used no model.

JOACHIM: Don't mess it with me. These hips are nothing generic. Do you think me a cunt?

(*JOACHIM is staring at CRANACH.*)

CRANACH: No, I don't think you a –

JOACHIM: This is specific flesh, by Gad. I can taste it. Feel it. Smell it. I'll meet this model. Explore these hips.

(*He looks at the sketch, rubs his fingers over it.*)

Sweet little minge. Who is she?

CRANACH: No one you know.

JOACHIM: I shall know. Depravities even the Borgias...! God-damn! Fetch her.

(*CRANACH looks at JOACHIM, shocked.*)

I'll pay you triple what the painting's worth.

CRANACH: You think me a Pander?

JOACHIM: You deal in goods.

CRANACH: I have erred in the drawing.

JOACHIM: Quadruple what the painting costs. Erred, he says. Four –

CRANACH: Hundred gulden...

JOACHIM: All you have to do is bring the girl.

CRANACH: There are complications.

JOACHIM: Of course there's complications! Why do you think I'm offering four hundred gulden? Keeps implying I'm some species of cunt. Yes, you'll have to work a bit for the money.

(*CRANACH thinks.*)

CRANACH: I just don't see how. Give me twenty-four hours?

(*JOACHIM grabs CRANACH, hugs and kisses him.*)

JOACHIM: Dear old chap, ain'tca?

CRANACH: I...

JOACHIM: Can I hang on to this?

CRANACH: A free gift.

JOACHIM: Make any... arrangements... with my man...

(*JOACHIM goes to the door, opens it and shouts out.*)

Benno!

(*To CRANACH*) Give him a time and place for delivery of the goods.

(*BENNO arrives at the door. JOACHIM ushers him in.*)

The painter has pleased me. Little extra business I'm throwing his way. Additional purchase.

(*JOACHIM winks. BENNO looks quizzically at CRANACH.*)

CRANACH: Your master wants delivery of a girl.

(*BENNO stares at CRANACH. JOACHIM looks at the sketch, whistles, grins, walks off. BENNO and CRANACH hold their gaze.*)

END OF ACT ONE

Act Two

17

(Outside the Inn. Bags are piled at the roadside. AVA and LUCAS stand by them. They hug each other tight. AVA breaks the hug.)

AVA: How soon will you forget me?

LUCAS: How soon do you think?

AVA: Soon as you lose sight of my waving arm.

LUCAS: No.

AVA: As soon as you pass the city gates.

LUCAS: Nope.

AVA: When you're on the highway.

LUCAS: Nah.

AVA: By the time you reach the first watering post.

LUCAS: This all goes to show how little you know.

AVA: You're bound to forget a know-nothing easy enough.

LUCAS: You know when I will forget you?

AVA: When?

LUCAS: When they tip me in the pit.

AVA: What pit is that, your bed back home in Wittenberg?

LUCAS: The only way to stop your nonsense is to –

(*He kisses here. She responds. They kiss long and deep. They stop kissing.*)

AVA: Kisses are easily forgot.

(*LUCAS sighs in frustration.*)

LUCAS: The painting will take no more than a week to turn around. Time to get there, time to return... I'll be no more than a fortnight.

AVA: A fortnight's plenty of time to meet a next girl.

LUCAS: How could any other woman warrant my eyes with your painting taking shape before me?

(*They kiss again.*)

Hated you posing for Dad.

AVA: It weren't so bad.

LUCAS: It was torture.

(*BENNO enters, observes them canoodling.*)

BENNO: Your father says that you might as well go back in your room for a bit.

(*The lovers spring apart.*)

I'm sure you'd both like a bit –

LUCAS: You want another lamping?

BENNO: Of time together before you go.

(*AVA glares at him.*)

	The cart to take your things to the coach stop's delayed.
LUCAS:	He's embarrassed at us being so ostentatious on the streets.
BENNO:	What passes in Proddie towns isn't appropriate here.
LUCAS:	(*To AVA*) Herr fish face is surly today.
AVA:	Let's go in for that bit.
LUCAS:	Let's make memories for my journey.

(*They run in, almost knocking CRANACH over as he is coming out whilst they rush into the Inn. They giggle at this. CRANACH approaches BENNO.*)

CRANACH:	That's the girl your Elector must de-flower.
BENNO:	Your son seems attached to her.
CRANACH:	Life throws us into tricky scrapes.
BENNO:	Doesn't it just.
CRANACH:	I want Lucas to be happy. Don't suppose her folk are anything much.
BENNO:	Don't suppose.
CRANACH:	You're awfully judgemental for a henchman.
BENNO:	I don't pretend to be other than a vessel of my master's will.

CRANACH: All of us hirelings.

BENNO: There's me thinking you an artist.

CRANACH: I paint for the market. Which is not to say I disavow meaning in my –

(*BENNO looks at CRANACH with distrust. CRANACH shrugs.*)

All must fall.

BENNO: Your trademark, I notice, is a serpent.

CRANACH: An identity for the brand. Don't read too much into it.

BENNO: I don't read.

CRANACH: Art can be read by illiterates.

BENNO: I know nothing of art.

CRANACH: Of craft?

BENNO: I'll take the girl home with me.

CRANACH: Tell her there's a treat in store. A trip to meet someone important.

BENNO: Isn't a lie...

CRANACH: Tell her she's meeting someone whose blessing she must obtain before I approve her marrying my son.

BENNO: Should egg her on.

CRANACH: I'm not imagining, am I? Your comments have an edge.

(*BENNO says nothing.*)

Eloquence of silence. You deliver the goods. The rest is – how shall we say? – the world's customary tale.

BENNO: She'll get no rest tonight.

CRANACH: Bawdy now, is it? Still with a cutting edge. The Elector shall have his way. Nearly said wicked way.

BENNO: Sedition.

CRANACH: Wild way. Like a boar and she'll be... torn, bruised and forlorn.

BENNO: You picture it all?

CRANACH: My mind creates pictures I don't draw. Pictures critical of power. Pictures are goods. Goods go to market. Where would the market for such pictures be?

BENNO: Proddies talk much of this market.

CRANACH: Beauty always finds a buyer. Moral lessons too. Make the consumer feel upright. The market likes functional things.

BENNO: Your pictures hung on a wall. A lass thrust against one.

CRANACH: A dark wall shall loom behind Lucrece. Flesh pale as milk. Vulnerable to curdling. Translucent chemise. Spirit. Easily besmirched. Knife in her mitt. Eyes sad. Head at a tilt. Looking. At you. A journeyman can do the wall. I'll take care of the face. Where is my sketchbook!

(*CRANACH scrabbles for his sketchbook. BENNO looks at him, full of contempt. BENNO leaves. CRANACH sketches.*)

*

18

(*The peasant hovel. AVA sits hunched before the fire, gazing into the flames. GRETEL shivers in a chair. BENNO paces.*)

BENNO: Go to bed, mother.

GRETEL: As if I could sleep tonight! Confounded by a thousand fears.

(*AVA turns to BENNO.*)

AVA: If you don't bring me?

BENNO: The Elector expects delivery tonight.

GRETEL: Say you lost her?

AVA: I could have run off.

BENNO: I'd be hung.

(*Pause.*)

AVA: Can't get my head around the painter. He knows how me and Lucas…

GRETEL: He'd never let the likes of you marry his son.

BENNO: Money's all that matters to Proddies.

AVA: He said such gentlemanly things.

GRETEL: Syrupy tongues reach for parts no other tongue has reached.

BENNO: Mother!

AVA: She's right. It was flattery.

(*BENNO starts crying.*)

Don't grizzle, please.

BENNO: I've failed.

GRETEL: A man of humble birth risen to Elector's right hand?

BENNO: I should protect her.

AVA: My father should be keeping me out of trouble.

GRETEL: What sort of a father was he? Couldn't keep himself out of... scrapes.

(*BENNO weeps more.*)

BENNO: I failed as a brother!

AVA: Where is dad?

(*BENNO wails.*)

GRETEL: If he was here, what could he do? Electors can do as they like.

BENNO: Your father would only make things worse. Get himself –

(*He stops, hangs his head in sadness.*)

GRETEL: For the best he's not here.

AVA: (*To BENNO*) Why did you never marry?

GRETEL: Look.

AVA: What?

GRETEL: At him.

AVA: What?

GRETEL: The face. What woman in their right mind?

BENNO: Nice to know I have your support, mother.

AVA: They say there's someone for everyone.

GRETEL: His Dad tried to buy him a bride once. We saved. His Dad found a girl. She was plain. Her parents were poor. She took one look at him. Her face, there was a picture! A week later we were informed she'd run away.

BENNO: No need to enjoy it so much.

AVA: What have you done for –

BENNO: What?

AVA: Go down the stews, do you? I don't blame you. Come on, admit –

BENNO: I don't see how the conversation has suddenly turned from your immanent ravishment to a discussion of whether or not I visit whores. The Elector will have you tonight unless we think of something.

AVA: We can't.

GRETEL: Let's pray to the Lord.

(*The nod. Rosaries are handed out by GRETEL and the three of them sit and pray. After a bit, AVA looks up.*)

AVA: The Elector's ever so powerful, isn't he?

(*The other two stop their prayers.*)

BENNO: Runs this manor. Like that with Rome. You know why they call him Elector?

(*She shrugs.*)

He's one of them elects the Emperor.

(*AVA wants to say something, daren't. GRETEL looks at AVA. GRETEL gets it.*)

GRETEL: It might do her some good.

(*BENNO is shocked.*)

Hasn't done you any harm, has it? Your association with him.

AVA: Paid to do his dirty work.

GRETEL: Regular meals on the table.

AVA: Buys evenings at the stews.

BENNO: I didn't admit that I go to the stews!

AVA: Something to admit then?

BENNO: Shut your faces.

AVA: I'm to be cast in a river. The current's strong. Let it carry me?

GRETEL: You might like where you end up. Who knows? You please men. You pleased the painter's son.

AVA: He wants to marry me.

GRETEL: He won't marry you. The arms of a Prince protect.

(*BENNO stares at them. GRETEL notices.*)

              What?

BENNO: I can see where my brother got it from.

AVA: (*To GRETEL*) Help me prepare.

(*The women lay aside their rosaries. GRETEL gets up.*)

GRETEL: I've some material I was saving. Thought for your wedding.

AVA: Thoughts of marriage away!

GRETEL: I'll run something up.

(*They leave the room. BENNO calls after them.*)

BENNO: The devil with both of you!

(*BENNO stares into the fire.*)

*

19

(*A hall in the Schloss. JOACHIM and ALBERT are polishing off an almighty meal. ALBERT speaks as he gorges on a fat capon.*)

ALBERT: Concerning those things you'd occasion to bring up in your confession...

(*He bites, munches, tucks in and so on throughout.*)

JOACHIM: They are supposed to be left in the confessional.

ALBERT: It is good for a man not to touch a woman.

JOACHIM: Better to touch one.

ALBERT: Facetious.

JOACHIM: That capon's juice makes rivers down your chin. You think that's good?

ALBERT: Let everyman have his wife and every woman her husband.

JOACHIM: I had a wife. I was properly had.

ALBERT: The husband gives to his wife due benevolence – nice euphemism – and the wife gives it to the husband.

JOACHIM: Monk Luther shouldn't have had a wife. He reformed that. He's wed. Muggins here is left.

ALBERT: "Better to marry than to burn." That's the clap. Scolds as you piss.

JOACHIM: You don't marry, do you?

ALBERT: Would that all men were as I.

JOACHIM: Doers with boys?

(*ALBERT chokes on his capon.*)

Not the first time you've choked on a capon's wish bone, eh?

ALBERT: None of your concern.

JOACHIM: Great example of celibacy, you are.

ALBERT: What I do doesn't jeopardize the state.

JOACHIM: One law for one –

ALBERT: You're Elector. You've responsibilities. You like the perks enough.

JOACHIM: What are your perks? Beardless varlets?

ALBERT: You fuck the printer's wife, Brandenburg'll be Lutheran by Christmas.

JOACHIM: And Luther's success has nothing to do with priests practising vices?

ALBERT: His followers were arsed off with our selling indulgences. They're tradesmen. They'd rather people spent money on their goods.

JOACHIM: You sell indulgences here. You endanger Brandenburg more than I!

ALBERT: How else do I keep the cathedral up to scratch?

JOACHIM: I will fuck. I cannot not fuck. And fuck you if you think I can fucking go without!

ALBERT: Your mouth's a swamp.

JOACHIM: Berlin's a swamp. I'm stuck in it. Up to my guts. I'll wallow. Flick my tongue out. Big fat toad. Fetch back a juicy bug.

ALBERT: These indulgences. I need to pay the Fuggers back the loan on the Cathedral.

JOACHIM: Fuggers? Fuck 'em. Bloody bankers. You know how much they make off me?

(*BENNO enters.*)

ALBERT: We're in the same boat. The crippling interest –

(*BENNO whispers in JOACHIM'S ear. JOACHIM nods, turns to ALBERT*)

JOACHIM: Leave me alone.

ALBERT: We haven't finished.

(*But JOACHIM has risen.*)

JOACHIM: The tabor player's available for a private gig in your room.

ALBERT: You've a woman lined up for yourself, haven't you?

JOACHIM: The tabor player's brought his brother to accompany him on the hautboy.

ALBERT: Brandenburg's future hangs like baggy stays on the legs of a harlot. Please say it's not the printer's wife. Older or younger brother?

JOACHIM: Younger.

(*ALBERT thinks for a moment and then gets up.*)

ALBERT: I'll retire. Feeling bloated. Nice lie down. Music. David composed psalms to a lute. His love for Jonathan was deep.

(*He goes. JOACHIM turns to BENNO.*)

JOACHIM: Where?

BENNO: Second bedroom on the third level. Second left as you leave the spiral staircase. In the third tower.

JOACHIM: A very nice room. Impress 'em with pomp and legs fly open like Cathedral doors on Easter Sunday.

(*Exit JOACHIM and BENNO.*)

*

20

(*A bedroom in the Schloss. GRETEL combs AVA's hair.*)

GRETEL: Not draughty. Big thick curtain. Lovely fire. Costs to heat a Schloss.

AVA: He can afford it.

GRETEL: The Elector's father once spat on your granddad. Your father saw it. One moment your granddad's face was grinning, pleased to witness his Lordship's presence. Next his beard was dripping with drool. His shamed old mug.

AVA: If Lucas knew –

GRETEL: His father will tell him. Anything to put the boy off.

AVA: You think about how you get from one place to another?

GRETEL: Stayed in the same place all my life.

AVA: These tapestries.

GRETEL: Swank.

AVA: Maiden with a posy.

GRETEL: Wild boar grunting.

AVA: Heralds and huntsmen.

GRETEL: Different world.

AVA: "Men who, since the Garden time, have lorded it o'er us in pomp and splendour. Lived off our losses. Strangled our gains. Blocked from their brothers a better age…"

GRETEL: Your Daddy's not coming back, Ava.

AVA: Where is he?

GRETEL: Somewhere he's not thinking of you.

AVA:　　　　Not true.

GRETEL:　　God's honest truth.

(*A great knock on the door. AVA stands up.*)

　　　　　　　Are you ready?

AVA:　　　　Enter destiny.

(*JOACHIM enters the room with BENNO. AVA and GRETEL face them.*)

JOACHIM:　Who's the old crone?

BENNO:　　This, sire, is a gentlewoman relation to the young lady.

JOACHIM:　Sod off, Memento Mori. I need youth. Give her coin.

BENNO:　　This way, crone.

GRETEL:　　I'll give you crone.

(*She hits BENNO. JOACHIM laughs.*)

　　　　　　　A pleasure to meet you, my lord.

(*GRETEL curtsies to JOACHIM then leaves. JOACHIM turns to AVA.*)

JOACHIM:　The knock. A courtesy. My Schloss after all. Like the room?

AVA:　　　　The nicest I've seen.

JOACHIM:　Not saying much. She wants to call me rude. She dares not. Who are you?

BENNO: Name.

AVA: Ava.

JOACHIM: Ever so nice, our Ava. Prettier than the drawing because the drawing's face... Wasn't much of a face. Who are your people?

BENNO: Nobodies.

JOACHIM: You snob! Your Mummy and Daddy important to you, aren't they?

AVA: I haven't a Mummy,

JOACHIM: Have you a Dad?

AVA: Not sure where he is.

JOACHIM: Shall I be your Daddy?

(*Pause.*)

AVA: A Prince is father to his people.

JOACHIM: She's very good. Push off.

(*It takes a moment for BENNO to register this. He then responds with a small bow and goes to the door.*)

      Wait outside. If need you I'll call.

(*BENNO bows again and goes out, closing the door.*)

      What a git. How's the wine?

AVA: He is a git. I haven't tried the wine.

(*JOACHIM strides to a table, pours two goblets of wine.*)

116

JOACHIM: Waits to be instructed. Nice.

(*He holds a goblet out for her.*)

This is shaping up to be good.

(*AVA crosses to him, takes a goblet. They drink.*)

You like?

AVA: Lots.

JOACHIM: Plenty more where that came from.

(*He drains his glass, pours another.*)

Master Cranach, he captured some of your...
Your figure makes my eyeballs roll. An hourglass
waist. Don't like too big a pair. I do like breasts
obviously, otherwise I'd be like... Someone I
know likes boys. Don't look shocked, it takes all
sorts. Love a breast I can cover with a palm.
Scooped up wounded bird.

(*He lays a hand on her breast, completely covers it.*)

You quiver as the robin –

AVA: Excitement.

JOACHIM: Not fear?

(*He squeezes her breast.*)

If you deny me, I must force my way.

AVA: I intend to enjoy you.

JOACHIM: You do?

AVA: Excited.

(*His hand moves down.*)

JOACHIM: So you are.

(*He takes his hand away, smells it.*)

> Perfumes I've smelt from Araby but none compare –

(*She laughs.*)

> What?

AVA: Never known owt like this.

JOACHIM: What do you think of it?

(*AVA is an enigma.*)

*

21

(*A cell in the Schloss. ALBERT is praying.*)

ALBERT: Again! And I shall do it again. Indulgences for sin. Sin is indulgence. Wish I could scrape my flesh away. As one scrapes gamey meat from the carcass of a fowl. Shred myself. Mound of contagion. Broiling pot of lusting lard. Be gone!

(*He pauses, pants.*)

> They are tinkers. Demonic sprites! They lead me on. You know. You saw. From Your omniscience.

118

> That glint. That wink. That come on grin. You
> do know, old Know-it-all!

(*He genuflects furiously.*)

> Of what did the little foxes chat? Huddle.
> Cornered. Older speaking to the younger. Serious.
> Tips on how to seduce? Forgive them. Forgive
> me. Forgive my frail brother. Deliver us. Save us.
> Loss of –

(*He fiddles away with his rosary.*)

*

22

(*BENNO and GRETEL are in the corridor, outside of the room JOACHIM has AVA in. Groans and moans and shouts from within. His ear is pressed against the door.*)

GRETEL: So unhealthy.

BENNO: Such noises.

GRETEL: Course there's noises! It's why you want to hear them I don't know.

BENNO: I don't want to hear.

GRETEL: Yet you –

BENNO: Rude ram, to batter an ivory wall!

GRETEL: Anyone'd think you're getting off.

(*He comes away from the door.*)

BENNO: This reminds me of –

GRETEL: Let me guess.

BENNO: Afternoons he snuck in a girl –

GRETEL: Always back to his brother.

BENNO: Mornings sometimes and evenings too –

GRETEL: Same with her, harps on her father.

BENNO: Tipped me the wink to stay out for a while –

GRETEL: How can I ever forget?

BENNO: Threat in that wink. I stayed out. Just outside the door.

GRETEL: Don't boast about it.

(*BENNO goes back to the door.*)

BENNO: She's inherited his seed of sin. Sapling. Seedling. Seeded.

GRETEL: Sounds as if you'd like a go!

BENNO: Never.

GRETEL: No?

BENNO: I'm not like that!

(*Suddenly the door bursts open, JOACHIM spills out sending BENNO flying out of the way. GRETEL gasps and runs around the corner out of sight.*)

JOACHIM: This maid has undone me endlessly. I'm a maddened thing –

(*He sees BENNO sprawled on the floor.*)

What the heck?

BENNO: I –

JOACHIM: Enjoying an earwig?

(*BENNO hangs his head.*)

You spank one out?

(*BENNO shakes his head vociferously, "no".*)

Don't waste it. Insatiable. I know they say that about women but I've never met... I've fucked out six – Is it seven? – She's still not –

(*He points BENNO towards the door.*)

Get yourself in, man.

(*BENNO doesn't get it.*)

Don't start with your "no sloppy seconds." Your face, you must go without for yonks. I'd be grateful. Really.

(*He shows BENNO inside the room. BENNO teeters on the edge of the doorway.*)

I'll watch.

(*BENNO and JOACHIM stare at each other. JOACHIM pushes BENNO into the room, watches him inside.*)

My dear girl, you've worn out your prince. Now for your frog.

(*JOACHIM smiles at what he sees.*)

Crone. Know you're there. Don't be shy.

(*GRETEL peeps around the corner.*)

GRETEL: Sire, I –

JOACHIM: You train her? You're some bawd. Deserve gold.

GRETEL: We're a poor lot.

JOACHIM: She has a vocation.

GRETEL: She has?

JOACHIM: A fucking vocation.

*

23

(*The Schloss. A painting with a cloth hung over it is propped against a box with CRANACH and LUCAS stand by it. An easel lies nearby.*)

CRANACH: No value in damaged goods. More than once I thought she was done for. Coach lurched. Nearly pitched us into some filthy ditch. Why doesn't he fix the roads? The same when we had Papists. Never a penny on public works. Be sorry to see her go.

LUCAS: Never seen you do so much of the work yourself.

CRANACH: Like to keep my hand in.

LUCAS: Where do you reckon she is?

CRANACH: Help me with this.

(*Father and son set an easel up.*)

LUCAS: She'd should have been at the Inn to greet us. I sent a letter to your man in good time.

CRANACH: The Elector's man. My bones are aching. Such a journey.

(*LUCAS helps CRANACH straighten the easel.*)

LUCAS: He might not have passed on the letter?

CRANACH: How should I know?

(*LUCAS has wandered to the painting.*)

I can do that myself.

LUCAS: Have I ever damaged –

CRANACH: Who knows when butterfingers strike? No value in damaged goods.

(*CRANACH mounts the painting on the easel.*)

LUCAS: Should be here.

CRANACH: She'd only moan about her nose. "Too much fat around my tummy."

Women are unreliable. They tend to weaken men. I've painted mighty Hercules reduced to a fat old drag queen. She'll turn up. People do. Never get rid of them that easy.

(*LUCAS glares.*)

Joke!

(*Enter JOACHIM. BENNO lurks in the doorway behind him.*)

Ah, there you are! Well, here she is.

(*During the following, LUCAS makes his way slowly to BENNO.*)

JOACHIM: As good as your word, Master Cranach.

CRANACH: When I strike a bargain –

JOACHIM: Never doubted.

(*He looks to the canvas on the easel.*)

This is her?

CRANACH: Indeed.

JOACHIM: What's up with the veil? She turned Mohammedan?

(*CRANACH laughs obsequiously.*)

Shy of showing your work?

CRANACH: We veil so we may unveil.

JOACHIM: Oh yes. Much sport to be had in unveiling.

(*JOACHIM laughs. LUCAS is with BENNO.*)

LUCAS: You give her my letter?

(*BENNO remains stoic.*)

          Is she safe?

JOACHIM: Strip her off.

(*CRANACH places himself by the picture, ready to unveil it.*)

CRANACH: You know of course the tale of Lucrece.

JOACHIM: Wouldn't be lumbered with this picture else. My brother reiterates the moral precepts therein, etcetera.

LUCAS: Take me to her.

CRANACH: Having been ravaged by rude Tarquinius –

JOACHIM: He raped her. More than rude, wouldn't you say?

CRANACH: The only means she had to show the world that she didn't acquiesce –

JOACHIM: We all know. Get on with it. I don't know why she was so unyielding. Women these days it's knock knock, "come in!"

LUCAS: Is she well?

CRANACH: The only way was for her to take a dagger. This the moment before –

LUCAS: Where is she?

(*CRANACH whips the veil from the picture. A black background broken by a window onto a landscape with a rock to the left of*

Lucrece, who is painted from the thighs up, standing naked except for a translucent chemise which floats around her shoulders and arms; a golden chain droops around her shoulders and she wears a thick collar dripping with pearls. Her right hand holds a knife upwards towards her heart; her face tilts to the left, looks out at us. JOACHIM stares at the picture as LUCAS stares at BENNO.)

JOACHIM: Oh yes.

(He moves in closer, inspects the body.)

> That's the body. Slight. Apples. Alabaster. Torso for roaming hands. Landscape of contours. Into the sweet folding valley. Cruel dagger. She looks so –

(He studies the face.)

> Oh.

(He stares at the face.)

> Time's ruin. Beauty's wrack. Care reigns.

(He backs away.)

> The eyes. They follow you. Around the room, don't they? They say that's a sign of a good picture yet I've seen masterpieces, the eyes are looking anywhere but. An accusing look. That Tarquinius should so abuse nobility! Horrid to contemplate...

(JOACHIM contemplates the image. LUCAS follows BENNO'S gaze to the picture then looks back sharply at BENNO.)

LUCAS: Tell me where she is or I'll do you.

(*CRANACH approaches JOACHIM.*)

CRANACH: You like?

(*JOACHIM snaps out of his reverie.*)

JOACHIM: How unlike is art to its spring.

CRANACH: I hope there's reality in it.

JOACHIM: To think you took this body from a wretch what —

(*LUCAS springs round.*)

LUCAS: Wretch?

CRANACH: If you're satisfied with the picture —

(*But JOACHIM has stalked over to LUCAS.*)

JOACHIM: Your Dad introduced me to the girl —

CRANACH: I don't think —

JOACHIM: Always an eye on a sale. Won't be aiming a knife towards herself, that one. Don't look as if butter wouldn't melt. We all know that kind of girl.

LUCAS: The girl that stood for this?

CRANACH: He means another —

JOACHIM: No other girl! What tosh. Your Daddy gave her to my man. I met her. Fucked her. Been fucking her solid the past fortnight. Worn me out. But good sport.

(*He is looking at BENNO.*)

He knows. Confess.

BENNO: Sport enough.

LUCAS: Father?

CRANACH: (*To JOACHIM*) If you're pleased with the painting –

JOACHIM: This'll keep me on the path. Imploring. Accusing. Reproving. Invoice my treasurer. You're bloody great artist.

(*JOACHIM pats CRANACH'S shoulder, sweeps out.*)

LUCAS: Father?

CRANACH: Lucas.

(*LUCAS turns to BENNO.*)

LUCAS: You!

(*LUCAS grabs BENNO round the throat, chokes him. BENNO struggles, sinking to the ground.*)

CRANACH: Lucas. Think of the scandal. He's the Elector's –

LUCAS: Villain!

(*BENNO gurgles and suffocates. LUCAS strangles away.*)

CRANACH: What's this proving? Your manhood? Protecting her virtue? There's none to protect.

(*LUCAS strangles all the more. BENNO grabs his wrists, pulls the young man off of him.*)

BENNO: I've had just about as much –

(*BENNO pushes LUCAS off. LUCAS staggers.*)

LUCAS: Think I've finished?

BENNO: This past few weeks I've had it up to here.

(*LUCAS and BENNO square up. CRANACH watches, appalled.*)

CRANACH: Lucas, it's beneath you. He's a churl.

(*LUCAS goes to punch BENNO. He misses. BENNO thumps LUCAS in the face, hard. LUCAS reels, his nose bleeding.*)

Churls are rather good at fighting.

(*LUCAS comes back, punches BENNO. He hardly feels it, comes back thumping. LUCAS puts up some defence but BENNO is into his stride now.*)

BENNO: Villain, am I?

LUCAS: Detestable.

(*BENNO punches him.*)

Wretch.

(*Another punch from BENNO, right in LUCAS' face. LUCAS is on his knees.*)

CRANACH: Let bygones be bygones.

BENNO: You spoilt little brat.

(*He grabs LUCAS by the hair, punches him very hard. LUCAS cries in agony.*)

Lord knows I need this.

(*He strangles. LUCAS desperately tries to say something. BENNO relaxes his grip for a moment. LUCAS gasps.*)

LUCAS: Kill me.

(*BENNO looks down at him, like he might pity him. CRANACH breathes a sigh of relief. BENNO resumes to choke LUCAS. CRANACH prevaricates then cries –*)

CRANACH: Gold.

(*BENNO stares at CRANACH.*)

BENNO: You think you can buy anything.

CRANACH: The Elector's rewarding me well for –

BENNO: Keep your cash. And your whelp.

(*He throws LUCAS to the floor.*)

Wish I'd never set eyes on you. Sure the girl feels the same.

(*BENNO exits. LUCAS lies in a bloody pulp on the floor. He looks up at his father. CRANACH slinks, embarrassed. LUCAS looks up at his Dad.*)

LUCAS: You sold my world.

CRANACH: Debts.

LUCAS: That makes it alright?

CRANACH: Ask our bookkeeper.

(*LUCAS slumps, cries.*)

What do bookkeepers know of the heart?

LUCAS: You know how I felt –

CRANACH: Felt?

LUCAS: What?

CRANACH: Past tense.

(*LUCAS wails.*)

Just saying.

LUCAS: We were to marry.

CRANACH: I can't deny that this past tense thing's a relief.

(*LUCAS roars great tears.*)

I never approved. Be a hypocrite to pretend. You heard the Elector. Doesn't sound as if she put up much of a fight. No value in damaged goods.

(*LUCAS looks up at CRANACH with his bloody, bashed and battered face.*)

Lasses I once loved. In the month of spring. Summer unlocks their buds. That sort of lass. Your Mum...

(*LUCAS stares in his father's face.*)

Nothing much to look at. Fat dowry. Keeps good house. Couldn't have built the business without... Nothing to leave my sons. You've a bright future. Your brother's not a bad dauber but you're the chip off the old... Been impressed by your landscapes of late. Don't think your brother's health will last. It'll all be yours.

(*CRANACH helps LUCAS onto his feet.*)

Experience shapes the artist. Her face –

(*LUCAS gazes at the face in the painting.*)

Didn't like selling the girl. Does it damn me? I'll speak to Martin. Felt painted into a corner.

(*Both CRANACH and LUCAS are staring at the portrait.*)

I too gave my virtue to him.

(*He gestures at the picture.*)

I pass that skill to you.

(*LUCAS looks from the painting to his father's face.*)

LUCAS: Think I'll thank you?

CRANACH: You shall.

LUCAS: World's stabbed. Blood weeps. Tears from a gash. An ever bleeding... Makes women of us.

(*He wipes his eyes, limps around, begins to pack his father's things away.*)

Jolly inheritance. Think they'll write books about artists? I'll get a nod. After you. Grateful. You're right. This'll improve my art.

CRANACH: Worms in the maiden bud. Cuckoos in sparrows' nests. We get over things.

132

LUCAS: We live in Christ's wounds.

CRANACH: Poor partner in pain.

(*CRANACH cradles LUCAS.*)

LUCAS: I'll weep when you die, daddy. And be a little glad. You didn't make this world a better place.

(*CRANACH nods and opens his arms; LUCAS collapses weeping into them. CRANACH strokes him as he cries, walks him off. Enter AVA. She looks around, tentatively walks up to the picture. She looks at it. She gasps. She moves in for a closer look. She looks and looks. Enter GRETEL.*)

GRETEL: Well?

(*AVA jumps.*)

AVA: What?

GRETEL: You're jumpy. What do you think?

(*AVA goes back to staring at the painting.*)

               Face nothing like you. All of... that... though. Is.

AVA: It's hard to –

(*She suddenly makes as if to vomit. GRETEL hands AVA her bag.*)

GRETEL: Here.

(*AVA vomits into the bag. GRETEL stares at the painting.*)

               Makes a change from the saints and Our Lady. I never liked a crucifixion.

AVA: I don't think He did.

GRETEL: Feel better now?

(*AVA vomits into the bag again.*)

        Wants to be careful with that knife. Do herself a mischief.

(*AVA seems to have stopped vomiting. She looks wretched. GRETEL takes her bag, closes it.*)

        You're not...?

(*GRETEL gestures her belly.*)

AVA: No.

(*GRETEL nods. AVA looks at the painting.*)

        Where's my face?

GRETEL: At least we can afford a new bag.

(*GRETEL leads AVA out.*)

*

24

(*Schloss chapel confessional. ALBERT taking JOACHIM'S confession within it.*)

JOACHIM: I've sinned since we last –

ALBERT: Surprise, surprise.

JOACHIM: Fucked a girl.

ALBERT: Who?

JOACHIM: Poor citizen.

ALBERT: Married?

JOACHIM: Young for marriage. Not that young! Older than your boys.

ALBERT: Whose daughter?

JOACHIM: Don't know.

ALBERT: Anyone important?

JOACHIM: Peasant.

ALBERT: Venial sin.

(*JOACHIM sighs in relief.*)

Spit in the spittoon, not on the fur rug. Where is she now?

JOACHIM: The Inn. Gave her twenty groschen.

ALBERT: And you with such debts...

JOACHIM: Set her up. Entertainment for guests. My penance?

ALBERT: The twenty groschen is paid. Anything else?

(*JOACHIM shakes his head, "no".*)

Give thanks to the Lord for He is good.

JOACHIM: For His mercy endures forever.

(*They step out of the confessional.*)

What do you think of Lucrece?

ALBERT: She's very good.

JOACHIM: That face!

ALBERT: A warning.

JOACHIM: To wound such a virtuous Lady! Tarquinius was scum.

ALBERT: Stick with wenches what don't matter.

(*They walk off.*)

*

25

(*BENNO at the crossroads. The corpse of his brother now a skeleton.*)

BENNO: You've lost weight. I clap it on. Round the belly. Regular job. Wage. Grub. Stuffed boar. Flagon of ale.

(*He rubs his neck.*)

A crick. Not as bad as yours. Had a brawl. Spare you the details.

(*He shivers.*)

Mum's alright. Drinks. Why shouldn't she? Misses you. I'm cold comfort. No use holding a grudge.

(*He stares at his brother.*)

> Your girl is fine. Try my best. Still dreams you'll return. Let her have her illusions. I've none. I count my blessings. One by one.

(*His brother's skeleton swings in the breeze.*)

*

26

(*1540. A nice enough room in town. AVA dressed in finery – posh dress, hair done lovely. GRETEL, also done up, drinking wine and admiring AVA's ostentatious new red hat.*)

GRETEL: Some might say it's showy.

AVA: Bitch gave me a right look.

GRETEL: Jealous.

AVA: Not like I don't work.

GRETEL: You work hard.

(*She puts the hat down. AVA pours drinks.*)

> Not much of a ceremony. Is that what the Proddies call a Mass? No nice smells nor chanting nor music nor nothing.

AVA: Nice being able to understand.

GRETEL: I like a bit of mystery. Who'd have thought it? Young Elector Joachim become a Reformer.

AVA: Don't he look serious?

GRETEL: His Dad's rolling in his grave.

AVA: Old bees die. The young possess the hive.

GRETEL: What he done to you, hope he's rotting in hell.

AVA: Don't rake it all up.

GRETEL: What he done to your father.

(*AVA looks at GRETEL quizzically.*)

GRETEL: Time you knew. The old Elector hung your Dad.

(*GRETEL starts to cry.*)

AVA: Don't start grizzling. You'll get me going. Here.

(*AVA hands GRETEL a handkerchief.*)

GRETEL: Ta

(*GRETEL dabs her eyes.*)

    Your Daddy never cared for you, Ava.

AVA: He did.

GRETEL: Ava –

AVA: Said I was special.

GRETEL: Dreams.

AVA: I am. I'm Lucrece. How many can say they're in art?

GRETEL: I wonder what your man'd say?

AVA: Who?

GRETEL: Son of the painter.

AVA: What about?

GRETEL: The young Elector going over to his side.

AVA: Haven't thought about him in donkey's.

(*AVA and GRETEL drink.*)

His dad painted the face so it wasn't my face. My body nonetheless.

GRETEL: No mistaking your body.

AVA: Captured it.

GRETEL: Look at you now. Nice gaff. All these goods.

AVA: Drink up. I've a client on the hour.

(*GRETEL readies to go.*)

GRETEL: I'll give your uncle your regards.

AVA: Did I hand you any to give him?

GRETEL: He's a broken man, Ava.

AVA: I done better than him. Better than you. Better than dad.

(*She remembers somebody's past words.*)

"Each generation improves on the last -

(*GRETEL stares at her, mystified.*)

- and, at last, The Golden Age blooms!"

139

GRETEL: That's Proddie talk, Ava.

AVA: The Protestants are right. We don't need Pope when we have a comfortable home, coin, and goods. God's blessings.

(GRETEL kisses her teeth, gets up heavily, struggles with her shawl. AVA helps her on with it. AVA kisses GRETEL goodbye. The old woman leaves. AVA sits waiting for her next client.)

THE END